"*Hearing God* is a book for our times. If they had asked me to subtitle it, I might have even suggested *Hearing God for Dummies*. And I mean that in the best way possible. I've always been a fan of demystifying all things God and religion—and that is exactly what my friend Nathan has done with this effort. He completely hits the mark. As followers of Jesus, we all too often remember that the message should be accessible for everyone but forget that our language can create barriers to understanding God in ways He never intended. Nathan's courageous attempt to explain this overwhelming but very real rhythm of faith is a guide we didn't know we needed."

—JUDAH SMITH, lead pastor of Churchome
and *New York Times* best-selling author of
Jesus Is _____.

"*Hearing God* is a guidebook for those seeking to better hear what God is saying to them. Nathan Finochio teaches us to find confidence in belonging to God and to be led by the Spirit. He cuts through many myths to reveal a biblical foundation for a personal relationship with Jesus. He grounds the reader in the truth of God's Word and debunks the myths often perpetuated through isolation, toxic community, and religion. You will be convinced that the Holy Spirit is seeking to speak to you in so many different ways and awakened to the many routes God takes to captivate your heart."

—RICH WILKERSON JR., pastor of VOUS Church
and author of *Friend of Sinners*

"Nathan Finochio candidly points our souls toward connection with our creator in *Hearing God*. He addresses the real questions of our hearts—even the questions we rarely voice—with genuine care and biblical insight. You will be encouraged with every chapter and will find yourself reflecting on every part of your life through the biblical lens Nathan so practically and generously shares with us."

—DAWNCHERÉ WILKERSON, pastor of VOUS Church

HEARING GOD

ELIMINATE MYTHS.
ENCOUNTER MEANING.

HEARING GOD

NATHAN FINOCHIO

WATERBROOK

HEARING GOD

Details in some anecdotes and stories have been changed to protect the identities of the persons involved.

Trade Paperback ISBN 978-0-7352-9171-3
eBook ISBN 978-0-7352-9172-0

Cover design by Matthew Scorte

Published in the United States by WaterBrook, an imprint of Random House, a division of Penguin Random House LLC.

WATERBROOK® and its deer colophon are registered trademarks of Penguin Random House LLC.

Library of Congress Cataloging-in-Publication Data
Names: Finochio, Nathan, author.
Title: Hearing God : eliminate myths, encounter meaning / Nathan Finochio.
Description: First Edition. | Colorado Springs : WaterBrook, 2019.
Identifiers: LCCN 2018047785| ISBN 9780735291713 (pbk.) | ISBN 9780735291720 (electronic)
Subjects: LCSH: Spirituality—Christianity. | Listening—Religious aspects—Christianity. | Communication—Religious aspects—Christianity.
Classification: LCC BV4501.3 .F56923 2019 | DDC 231.7—dc23
LC record available at https://lccn.loc.gov/2018047785

Printed in India

10 9 8 7 6 5 4

SPECIAL SALES
Most WaterBrook books are available at special quantity discounts when purchased in bulk by corporations, organizations, and special-interest groups. Custom imprinting or excerpting can also be done to fit special needs. For information, please email specialmarketscms@penguinrandomhouse.com.

For Jasmine—the clearest
voice of God I've ever heard

Contents

Introduction

Have you ever felt like you're just not as "spiritual" as every-
one else? I don't mean that you believe less or feel less, just that
your number doesn't seem to be saved in God's contacts.

You have friends who seem to be on speed dial with Him.
Favorites. They're always talking about how "God just told me . . ."
or something great and intimate and personal like that. You find
yourself politely nodding as you sit there and blink. You'd love to
experience that, but you half wonder if it's even possible. And as
they go on and *on,* you also start wondering if what they're talking
about is even real. They seem to have their heads in the clouds half
the time, anyway.

But then you have a moment in heartfelt worship, or come
across a story or verse in the Bible, or some social media post that
makes you long for something. It's a moment of meaning or
beauty that almost feels like *God said something to you.* Then it's
gone, leaving you wanting more.

I'm writing this book because we need to talk about hearing

God for the rest of us—for the people who struggle with it. Who want it but don't quite know how to sort out what's real or what's true among the conflicting ways Christians talk about it. If you want more and you don't quite know how to find it, this book is for you.

In some ways I'm exactly who you'd expect to write a book like this: a pastor and a worship musician. But in other ways I'm not. I've had to struggle to come to my own understanding of how God speaks to us.

Here's the thing: if God is really speaking to His people, then the most important things we can do are to stop, learn, and listen. We need to *stop* what holds us back, *learn* what can move us forward, and then simply *listen* to what He's saying. He's not trying to make this hard. He's not playing games. But getting to a place where we can hear Him with clarity and confidence does require growth from us.

My prayer is that you'll walk in freedom as together we step into an understanding of this world as a place where God's talking. Like, *a lot.* That's what this book is about—how God is speaking through all kinds of channels. He's probably speaking to you right now, but you don't even recognize it's Him!

Every one of us buys into some sort of myth about God's voice and how to hear it. With that in mind, I've divided this book into the myths we believe about each of the big ways of hearing and the truths that can smoosh those myths like a Philistine between Samson's sweet anointed pecs.

So I guess I'm saying there's good news. God's voice is closer than we think, and He wants us to hear Him. You don't need to buy oil from Israel or blow a shofar to hear God. You don't need to hang out at a hip church. You don't need a PhD in theology. You don't need to wear a leather jacket and skinny jeans. You don't need to become a hermit. You don't need to become a televangelist. You can be *you*. I can be *me*. In fact, that's exactly how God wants it.

We don't need to change who we are, but we do need to change how we listen.

CHAPTER ONE

The Myth of Easy Conversation

Good Grief! Why Is It *So Hard* Sometimes to Just Communicate?

When they had come together, they asked him, "Lord, will you at this time restore the kingdom to Israel?" He said to them, "It is not for you to know times or seasons that the Father has fixed by his own authority. But you will receive power when the Holy Spirit has come upon you, and you will be my witnesses in Jerusalem and in all Judea and Samaria, and to the end of the earth." And when he had said these things, as they were looking on, he was lifted up, and a cloud took him out of their sight.

—Acts 1:6–9

Sometimes when my wife, Jasmine, talks to me, I feel a bit like a conversational Indiana Jones. Deep beneath the ancient sands, I'm trying to make out the hieroglyphics that hold the information I need. *The secret must be here!* I think, frantic. *The treasure!*

For example, let's say she says "Whatever." This does *not* mean a casual "Whatever," like the "Whatever" one of my guy friends employs when I ask what movie we should watch or where we should grab a bite. When Jasmine says "Whatever," it means that I have somehow, in some way, failed miserably and that I need to retrace my steps and *immediately* make further inquiry to determine what I'm repenting for.

In this example, I ask what's wrong, and she responds with "Nothing." What she's really saying is precisely the opposite, that there *is* indeed something wrong and that I'm in a relational minefield. Explosives are hidden, and I must throw out every possible "Is it . . . ?" or "Did I . . . ?" scenario until I hit the mine. *Boom.*

Now let's say that Jasmine answers "It's fine." With the correct tonal inflection, this means *nothing* is fine. Everything has gone to the dogs. The world is about to end. I brace for impact and begin to apologize for anything that comes to mind, including the sins of my childhood.

Admittedly, we've been married for only five years, and we do still have a ton to learn about communication. But we *are* learning, slowly. It's not that Jasmine is bad at communicating; she's great. And it's not that I'm bad at listening. But I'm still learning to listen to *her*. She's not a high-maintenance person—quite the opposite. Our goal is to converse more effectively. Why is that necessary? Because we're different as people.

The good news is that difficulty doesn't doom possibility. As my relationship with Jasmine grows, so does my understanding of how she talks. How she expresses herself is not what I am used to. *Okay. Buck up, Nathan!*

Through time spent, understandings, and misunderstandings, I've had to unlearn certain meanings of words and tones and learn Jasmine's. And she's had to learn mine. It's taking longer than I had hoped, but it's happening in the context of relationship, and it's clarifying over time. I'm still not perfect, and I still have a long way to go. That process of "two becoming one" and "blending" plays out over a lifetime. But in the end—if we're diligent— I'm sure we'll be finishing each other's . . .

Sandwiches.

Here's the point: conversation grows as we do. Maturity and experience are linked to communication. If Jasmine and I get to our fiftieth wedding anniversary and we're still exactly where we were at our fifth, something's wrong. Why? Because relationships should grow.

There are two myths about conversation that bite at the very foundation of hearing God. One is that hearing God is all about *me*. The other is that it is all about *Him*. The truth is that it's about *both*, like any conversation is.

If a conversation is all about the will, needs, wants, and life of one person, it's a monologue. Yet that's how many of us think about our conversations with God. Either they're all about us (this kind of crazy focus on me, me, me) or they're all about Him (this kind of crazy focus on theology and His will that never considers that we're real people too). Both views are immature on our part.

What's the goal in hearing God? Just as in marriage, it's balance. Just as in marriage, it's mutual understanding. Just as in marriage, it's *conversation*.

It's All Who You Know

Hearing God begins with relationship. Consider the type of revelation John the apostle had about Jesus and relate that to his proximity to Jesus. John was probably Jesus's best friend. He was the last of the twelve disciples at the cross and the first one at the grave. John took care of Jesus's mother, Mary, after Jesus's death—at Jesus's request. John laid his head on Jesus's breast at the Last Supper. Five times in his gospel, John calls himself the one whom Jesus loved. It was his identity. And in this gospel, we have the most intimate glimpse of Jesus. About 80 percent of the material is also unique, telling us things the other three gospels don't. We get an in-depth, transparent picture of Jesus—aside from what we see in the incredible (and terrifying) book of Revelation, which begins with a vision of Jesus in crazy power and glory.

It's easy to hear all that and think *Goody for John. Must be great. So . . . what am I supposed to do?* Here's what: Start by understanding that Jesus desires closeness and intimacy with you. Understand that, through the Holy Spirit, that kind of relationship is possible, and that just as in relationships with friends and spouses, that relationship can grow in intimacy.

If that's true, then there's hope for each of us to learn how to hear what God is truly saying. We *can* understand. He *wants* us to. But don't take *my* word for it.

To begin with, read the Acts passage that opens this chapter. Jesus, resurrected, reveals Himself to the disciples and hangs out with them over a period of forty days, speaking about the kingdom of God (Acts 1:3). Don't you wish they had recorded that discussion? Think about it. The risen Jesus is doing some crazy explaining to the disciples, filling in the gaps of what they didn't understand about His death and resurrection. Not only has He been with these guys for more than ~~three~~ one years—healing people, walking on water, showing them unparalleled signs, and telling secrets about Himself—but now He's just been raised from the dead. He is Next-Level Jesus; He is Death-Defying Jesus; He is Walk-Through-Walls Jesus. And He's explaining both Himself and the kingdom of God to them in a fuller, more robust way. All this is amazing, but what happens next is mind blowing.

Here's how the Finochio Amplified Version tells the story:

They're all at some secret, Jesus-followers-only location, and Jesus is thinking, *Perfect—I've just come back from the dead and have spoken to my future church planters about the kingdom at length. They get it! Now I'm gonna go to the Father. Everything is perfect—mission accomplished.*

Jesus looks down at the ground, about to engage thrusters and blast off into the clouds, but just as He says *Launch!* internally and begins to lift into the air, the disciples grab His ankles and yell, "Wait! We have one more question!" Jesus is four feet off the ground, and they're holding Him like small children gripping clusters of helium-filled balloons.

Okay—so maybe it wasn't *quite* like that. Just humor me for a minute.

Hovering above the sand, Jesus answers, "What is it? What could I have possibly left out?"

The disciples answer, "Lord, will You at this time restore the kingdom to Israel? Is that what You're floating off to do? Destroy the Romans and Herods in an air assault? Should we meet You at the palace or temple, where You'll assume command of the country and sit on the throne of Israel as the rightful heir of the Davidic dynasty? And do we all get sweet rings of power and large country estates from which we rule and reign over our beloved country with You?"

Jesus sinks down like a deflated balloon and somewhat impatiently exclaims, "Look, it's not for you to know what the Father is doing with respect to all that stuff. And yes, you'll receive power—when the Holy Spirit has come upon you. Then you'll be My witnesses in Jerusalem and throughout the world. Like I said before, it's better that I go so that you have the Paraclete *holy spirit* with you. He's going to help you understand all this stuff you're a bit hazy on, and even more! I'm out of here, guys. Peace!"

After Jesus whips up into heaven, the disciples are all looking up like children who lost balloons, in a mix of befuddlement and grief. Two angels appear immediately as the guys are gazing into the distance, wondering what just happened.

"Guys? Um, Jesus is gone. What are you staring at? Jesus will return the same way, so maybe stop staring so hard at the clouds, 'cuz He isn't coming back right this moment. Go chill in Jerusalem and wait like He said."

The Gospels culminate in the total victory of Jesus and the almost-total failure of His disciples. The beginning of the book of Acts continues that narrative: Jesus is constantly explaining Himself and the kingdom of God to the disciples, and the disciples are constantly missing everything He's communicating. But that same book of Acts shows this formerly wavering, dense, and impulsive group transformed into bold leaders and witnesses through the power Jesus promised. God's fullest revelation of Himself is given to His friends, to those with whom He has close relationship. They are then asked to take it to others—everywhere. But it doesn't get off to the smoothest start, does it?

Here's the point: God isn't the problem when it comes to hearing Him; we are. In our minds we often put the burden of hearing God on God Himself. We walk around with our proverbial fingers in our ears or our cognitive and spiritual iPods on blast, and then we pray prayers like *God, speak to me!* But what if He *has* spoken to us? What if He *is* speaking to us? What if we're missing the point—and we have been for years?

My wife isn't an alien; she just doesn't think or speak the same way as I do. And the truth is that God doesn't think or speak the way I think or speak either. If I want to hear Him, I'm the one who must change, not Him. But most Christians treat God as they treat others: they place themselves at the center of the universe and demand that others and God adopt their modus operandi.

That's how the disciples are acting in this passage: their ears are completely incapable of deciphering Jesus's clear messages because they have an agenda that needs losing. Or better yet, they have a theology that needs losing.

I need to stop and say something important before we go on with this. You may have read the preceding few paragraphs and thought, *Yeah, I always knew the problem was with me. I knew I wasn't good enough. I always find a way to mess up everything. Why would my relationship with God be any different?*

Stop that. Right now. Would you expect a guy married for five years to be able to communicate with his wife as though they'd been married for fifty? Of course not. Would you expect a toddler just learning to walk to run a marathon? Of course not. You jump up and down and praise them when they make it from the coffee table to the couch. There's no shame and guilt in needing to grow.

Because God is so humble and so foolishly in love with us (who are unfaithful and hard-hearted), He constantly climbs down to our level (as He did when He took on the form of a bondservant), speaking to us right where we are—even in the middle of our distorted agendas.

John 21 is an incredible passage that illustrates Jesus's rhetorical descent to Peter's level. The depth of the exchange is easy to miss in English because there's only one word for "love." But the Greek language has four words—how nice! The first time Jesus asks Peter if he loves Him, Jesus uses the word for "unconditional" love, asking, "Do you *agape* Me?"

Peter replies *with a different word,* the one for "friendship love": "Yes, Lord, I *phileo* You."

Jesus asks again, "Peter, do you *agape* Me?"

Peter replies, "Lord, I already told You—I *phileo* You!"

Peter isn't getting the point, so Jesus descends to Peter's limited understanding of love and finally asks, "Peter, do you *phileo* Me?"

Peter replies, "Yes, Lord, I *phileo* You."

Like a parent speaking baby talk to a toddler, Jesus adapts how He's talking so that Peter will be on the same page with Him. This perfectly illustrates my point: the problem isn't the heart or mouth of God but the hearts and ears of humanity. We need to grow.

Fortunately, what we need is exactly what He wants.

Central Communication

This means that we don't need to find the perfect recipe to hear God, but we must be willing to grow and do our sincere best to listen for His voice and begin the conversation. We have important things to talk about, and so does He. So when we give up the paralyzing notion that our conversation is *just* us bringing a laundry list of prayer requests or *just* us waiting in silence for the clouds to part and His *perfect will* to descend inscribed on golden tablets, then we're beginning to get the point. This is a two-way conversation, in service of a growing relationship.

The Father must become central to our world if we're going to hear Him. If we think that it's all about us and our little world and that God must speak in our language, on our timetable, in our way, then we're going to be frustrated. We don't even approach celebrities this way, so why would we approach God Almighty that way?

Could it be that one of our communication problems is that we have an unbiblical idea about God? He's not Santa Claus, but many of us treat Him as though He is. Santa exists only for the child; there's no relationship there. He reads the child's list and does his yuletide magic, but he has no suggestions for toys that might be best for the rosy-cheeked little imps pestering him for gifts. Santa has no opinions, and it's a one-way conversation.

God is so much better. Santa is one dimensional and unimaginative and boring. He's a slave to our dull imagination. God invented imagination. He's in the business of abundantly giving what is truly good for us, not of satisfying our every whim. (And whims we have aplenty, eh?)

Ephesians 3:20 says God can do exceedingly, "abundantly," above all we could even ask or think. So why is what we ask Him to talk to us about often so limited? When I stop and think about it, I realize that I don't want God just to answer my small prayers and requests; I want Him to be good enough to do *more* than I ask. And He is. I don't want God to respond to my thoughtless moments; I want to be stretched. I want to grow until I can consistently put the focus on Him, allowing Him to reimagine me. I want to grow into a God-sized life, a God-imagined inheritance, and a God-dreamed relationship with a God-given language.

For this to happen, however, I must hop out of the conversational driver's seat. I can't fall into the temptation to jabber or believe that I don't have anything God wants to hear. I can't go to Him with my list and then assume something ridiculous about His character—that He's "silent," for example—when I don't hear what I want. Maybe I'm just not shutting up and listening, and He's too polite to interrupt most of the time. I need to find the happy balance that all conversations need to really get anywhere. I need to learn how He talks. And I need to share my heart.

God doesn't change (Malachi 3:6)—He's the same yesterday, today, and forever (Hebrews 13:8). I, however, change a *lot* and need to change even more. God is the anchored and steady one who is always good; I'm the unfaithful and unsteady one who is almost never totally in the right place. But He loves me anyway! So the first step to my hearing God more and better is understanding that need to grow. This isn't a shameful or necessarily sinful thing. It's natural to have to grow in understanding, just as it's natural for a kid to have to learn how to communicate in their first years. Dad doesn't learn to speak Toddler (though he can understand it pretty well); Toddler learns to speak Dad.

I'm Toddler. God is Dad. I must grow to hear Him more, to understand Him better.

Thankfully, the Acts 1 narrative doesn't leave us hanging. Even though Jesus's earthly ministry is finished in Acts 1 and the disciples still seem *so* far away from what He was trying to accomplish, the Holy Spirit comes in the very next chapter. In John 16:7, Jesus had even said this would be better for the disciples: "It is to your advantage that I go away, for if I do not go away, the Helper will not come to you. But if I go, I will send him to you."

Throughout his gospel John remarks that a lot of things Jesus said to him and the other disciples were unintelligible to them at the time, *but then later they made sense.* What does that mean? That they grew into their listening. The disciples were "learning" Jesus and had a staggering amount of "unlearning" to do. They had to unlearn their religiosity, and they had to unlearn the broken interpretation of the Scriptures their traditions had created. In the beginning they could catch every single word yet miss the point because they didn't have the framework to see and hear it.

Besides their natural process of maturing, the Holy Spirit had yet to come and "teach [them] all things" (John 14:26). Jesus continues talking about the Holy Spirit in John 16:13: "When the Spirit of truth comes, he will guide you into all the truth." Many of us think it would be easier if Jesus were here, right beside us every day, wearing His earth suit and whispering that "Footprints in the Sand" poem every time we feel confused. But Jesus explained in John 16 that we have an advantage in His being gone and the Holy Spirit being here. At the end of Acts 1, we see the disciples trying to figure out God's will by casting lots to see who will take Judas Iscariot's place on the disciple roster. In the next chapter, they all get filled with the Holy Spirit, and we never see lots cast again. Why? Because they now have the leading and direction of the Holy Spirit!

We're no different from the disciples. We need growth. We

need the Holy Spirit to lead us into deeper and deeper truth. Just like a toddler grows in his ability to talk Dad—or like I'm growing, year by year, in being able to understand Jasmine—we need to progress in how we hear God.

Those of us who have received the Spirit of God have an incredible advantage in *hearing* God, because one of the main roles of the Spirit is to teach us all things. He will help us understand God's Word and will. Let's talk through the steps typical for us to grow as we continue in the Holy Spirit.

Just Like Jesus

Hearing God is intimately tied to our relationship with the Holy Spirit. I think we tend to forget that Jesus was Spirit-filled, Spirit-led, and Spirit-dependent, just like us. So why don't we talk about the importance of the Holy Spirit in Jesus's life and ministry? Spirit-Filled Jesus seems to be pretty much missing from our teaching.

I mean, for starters, consider Jesus's birth: He was born of the Spirit. Don't ask me how that worked, but the Holy Spirit is His biological dad, not Joseph. Now link that idea up with Romans 8:15, which says, "You did not receive the spirit of slavery to fall back into fear, but you have received the Spirit of adoption as sons, by whom we cry, 'Abba! Father!'" If you're a Christian, the Holy Spirit has begun a work in your life by adopting you and making you part of the family. *Jesus's* family. You're Spirit-born—that's the starting point of your walk with God. Sure, it's a little different from the virgin birth, but the idea is meant to make you go, "Huh."

Check this: In Luke 4:14 we see a new dimension in Jesus's ministry after He'd been ministered to by the power of God and angels. After the wilderness, Jesus returned to Galilee "in the power of the Spirit."

With that truth in mind, we can feel confident that if the Holy Spirit has adopted us into God's family, we don't need to fear that God is going to abandon us or leave us high and dry. It's by the Holy Spirit that we pray, "Father, speak to me!" The Spirit is connecting us to the Father, making sure we're always tethered to His heart and mind.

Embracing this can transform your spiritual life. Knowing that you are the Father's daughter or son will mean that the fear of not being able to hear God or that you'll somehow miss His will can be thrown out the window! You are born of the Spirit and into the family, just like Jesus, your older brother, was. As you grow to look more like Him, you'll notice more similarities along the way.

Spirit-Born Jesus was baptized, and if you're a Christian, you ought to be baptized too. The Bible says that after Jesus's baptism, the Holy Spirit descended on Him in the form of a dove and an audible voice spoke from heaven, saying, "This is my beloved Son, with whom I am well pleased" (Matthew 3:17). Have you been baptized? If not, get dunked! It's a powerful way to connect to the reality that God wants you to walk the same way Jesus did—in surrender and relationship with Him. If you've already confessed Jesus as Lord and been baptized, you can have an incredible assurance that the Holy Spirit is not only in you but that the Father is speaking His Fatherly pleasure over your life. He loves you. He's pleased with who you are in your identity, unconditionally loving and delighting in you, apart from anything you do or don't do. (Although obviously He cares about what you do and don't do!)

Back to the point. The Bible says that immediately after His baptism, "Jesus, full of the Holy Spirit, returned from the Jordan and was led by the Spirit in the wilderness" (Luke 4:1). Baptized Jesus was then Spirit-Full Jesus and then Spirit-*Led* Jesus.

When I started writing this book several years ago, I felt that I needed to hear God (the classic preacher move—speak about what you're going through!). I felt as if I were in a wilderness, as if I couldn't hear. I wondered what the issue was. Maybe things weren't going the way I wanted them to because I hadn't made the right decisions. Maybe it was another person's fault (per the usual). Maybe it was the devil's fault (per the *even more usual*).

Luke 4:1 hit me right between the eyes. Strangely, it started bringing back my confidence. Even Spirit-Led Jesus found Himself in a desert. Testing and wilderness experiences don't mean that you've sinned, even if the devil is there. After all, he didn't lead Jesus there—the Spirit did. And if the Spirit led Spirit-Full Jesus to the desert, then that was the perfect place for Him to be at that time. Maybe it was for me too. Maybe I needed "the desert" to grow.

Part of what the Holy Spirit is trying to do in my life is mature me. Because the Holy Spirit is all about making us grow as members of the Father's family, the Holy Spirit will take us to the gym of life and teach us the workout routine. He'll show us the family business: being more than conquerors. Sometimes it takes a while. That's okay, because we can have incredible confidence knowing that we belong to the Father and that the Holy Spirit is leading us into the right places. We belong to the Father now. We don't have to fear when we know we belong to Him.

Yet we may say, *Father, I'm experiencing some serious challenges. Believe it or not, there are some things I cannot do. And I'm worried that I'm not part of the family because I haven't yet developed the muscle to be, and do, what I'm called to.*

God's voice to that fear is, *You're Spirit-born; you belong to Me. You're baptized, you're Mine, and I'm pleased. You're Spirit-full and Spirit-led, and you're going to grow into who and what I've called you to.*

I don't like wilderness. I don't like processes. I don't like remote regions. I don't like gyms and testing and push-ups and pull-ups and sit-ups and cardio and planking and all the horrible things the trainer makes me do. I like my will and my way and going to Disneyland with a stop at In-N-Out Burger, double cheeseburger with onions all the way. But I belong to the Father now, by the Spirit, and because He is a good Father, He puts me into the processes that will mature me and bring out the best in me.

I think we miss the specific God-word or God-thought for our lives because we become so ignorant of the ultimate. We forget what God is accomplishing. We start cursing what God is blessing; we think the Holy Spirit is the devil; we view the Trainer as the taskmaster.

I've found that I'm starting to like the gym, little by little. I'm starting to like eating healthily, little by little. I'm no longer calling leafy greens the devil's lettuce. I'm starting to thank God for what seem to be setbacks, and I'm not giving credit to the devil or demons or even my own weakness or others' idiocy. I'm beginning to thank God for what He's leading me into, because at the end of the day, I belong to Him and nobody can snatch me out of His hand. I'm Spirit-born, Spirit-baptized, Spirit-full, Spirit-led, and I'm right where I'm supposed to be. No fear.

Fresh Filling

When I sit down with a friend, I don't always have an agenda; the conversation may go in places I never thought of before. And when I'm sitting down to talk with people who have a lot of influence in my life, I let *them* set the pace. Sometimes they want to talk about things I haven't considered important, yet they see them critically missing from my life. I've learned not to crowd the conversation but to allow them the space to talk about what they consider timely.

This is how we need to go to God. Through all the ways He speaks, we need to let His Spirit lead. God has work in store for us; He knows exactly what we need to hear at the exact time we need to hear it. He knows all our needs before we even ask for His help. Just as Jesus yielded to the work of the Holy Spirit and allowed the Holy Spirit to set the pace and direction, so must we, or else we end up like the disciples, clueless about what Jesus is saying because we're so full of agendas.

Are you able to be led and clear your agenda? When was the last time you set aside time to be filled in a fresh way by the Holy Spirit? Or are you so full of agendas and timetables and topics that you need to discuss that you don't have time to "wait for the Lord" (Psalm 37:34)?

Wait on the Lord, and keep His way, and the shall exalt thee to inherit the land, when the wicked are cut off, thou shalt see it.

Just because you're Spirit-born doesn't mean you're Spirit-full. *Filled* doesn't mean "full." In Ephesians 3:19 Paul said that he was praying that the Ephesians "may be filled with all the fullness of God." Filled with all the fullness. There is one Spirit-birth when the Spirit comes to dwell in us, but there are many Spirit fillings when His power in us is increased or renewed. While Jesus was totally God, He was still dependent on the Holy Spirit for power in His earthly ministry and for His resurrection.

The world and the flesh and the devil will all attack your identity as a son or daughter, because if they can destabilize your core, you won't be able to hear God as your Father. You'll see His processes as provocations; you'll see the people He's brought into your life as limiters rather than limit lifters.

This opening chapter is a bit of a lens cleaner: it's meant to refresh how you're seeing God's sovereignty in your life and how you're seeing the Holy Spirit as a source of power. Luke 4:14 shows us a Spirit-powered Jesus. This new paradigm helped Him to hear the Father properly. Our lens with which we see and effectively hear God is vital. As we are solidified as a son or daughter, more of His speech is detected. The Holy Spirit brings a new degree of power to be a son or daughter as we walk this out.

Spirit-Powered Jesus becomes Spirit-Anointed Jesus in Luke 4:18. Jesus reads a passage in Isaiah about who He is and simultaneously fulfills it. Jesus's life and ministry and calling are all Spirit-dependent, and the Scriptures testified to them. As Jesus's identity is solidified and strengthened as a Son, now a clarity in His calling is solidified and strengthened.

What if you asked the Holy Spirit to fill you in a fresh way today? What if you asked the Holy Spirit to tell your heart again about how you belong to the Father? Maybe today you should ask the Holy Spirit to open your eyes and ears to the son or daughter work He's working in you. Ask Him to help you see what He's trying to shape in you and to open your ears and heart to these powerful, shaping words. Ask Him to tell you where they're coming from and who they may be coming from. Ask Him to give you patience with those voices. Ask Him for His power to receive those words and their formative authority. And as you begin to look back on your life, as John the Beloved did, you'll begin to have those moments when you're like, "Oh wow. That was God speaking to me the entire time, and I just didn't get it until now."

I'm telling you that God, by the Holy Spirit, is speaking His formative words over you from so many angles, but you're just not hearing them yet. You will, though. You'll recognize His patterns. You'll learn His language. You'll figure this out, and you'll grow.

Maybe what we need to do is lean in. Draw close. Ask the Holy Spirit to draw us to Himself, to show us who we are in Him. And then listen when we need to listen and speak when we need to speak.

Just like in a conversation.

 Remember: Hearing God starts by under-standing that He wants a *conversation* as part of a *growing relationship.*

CHAPTER TWO

The Myth of Technicolor Holy Spirit Wonkaland

Heck, Why Is God Even Talking to Me in the First Place?

We have much to say, and it is hard to explain, since you have become dull of hearing. For though by this time you ought to be teachers, you need someone to teach you again the basic principles of the oracles of God. You need milk, not solid food, for everyone who lives on milk is unskilled in the word of righteousness, since he is a child. But solid food is for the mature, for those who have their powers of discernment trained by constant practice to distinguish good from evil.

—HEBREWS 5:11–14

We know that for those who love God all things work together for good, for those who are called according to his purpose. For those whom he foreknew he also predestined to be conformed to the image of his Son, in order that he might be the firstborn among many brothers. And those whom he predestined he also called, and those whom he called he also justified, and those whom he justified he also glorified.

—Romans 8:28–30

Have you ever met hyperspiritual Christians who enjoy let-ting everyone know how in tune with God they are? I'm not talking about the people who really talk to God (I love *them*); I'm talking about the people who need you to know that they talk to God, like, all the time, and that He talks back, like, all the time, and that everything in their lives is a Technicolor Holy Spirit Wonkaland.

But who can blame them? A lot of well-meaning leaders care-lessly throw around spiritualized phrases all the time, such as "and then God told me to wear this suit" or "and then the Holy Spirit gave *me* a parking spot." Rather than encouraging real faith, these claims reinforce people's superstitions. And worse? Flippantly tacking "God told me" on to everything desensitizes us to what hearing God means.

I don't doubt that God has told many people strange things; I don't doubt many people have a special relationship with God and have attuned their ears to the Spirit's whisper. But I also don't think the Holy Spirit is constantly telling us what to eat for lunch, and I think some of the stories leaders tell about the Holy Spirit helping them with their shopping, or some other cute solution, paint an unhealthy and impossible portrait that (a) God speaks only to superspiritual people and (b) God is uniquely obsessed with finding His children great parking spaces.

Think about this for a second. Your spouse or best friend doesn't even want to tell you what to eat or where to park or what shirt to wear. Special occasion? Okay, maybe then they'll want to tell you what shirt to put on. But the point of being a person is sort of to *be a person*. To grow up. To make choices—sometimes great, sometimes less than great, usually in between.

Good parents don't have to tell their mature children what to eat. Why? Because the entire point of maturity is to release their kids into making solid choices for themselves. God wants you to know what you want and need, and then to order it off the menu.

The paradox of Christian maturity is at once an increased dependence and an increased independence. But it's not a given that we understand this. So many Christians are slamming their foreheads against the wall right now, crying out to God, *Lord! Where should I live?* And God is shouting back, *Dude! Where do you* want *to live?*

Of course God leads. Of course He guides. Of course He wants to be inquired of and consulted and in turn give counsel and wisdom and instruction. And *of course* He wants to build relationship through conversation in a million other ways. I'm not saying God doesn't want to be a part of our lives; I'm saying we settle for too little.

We'll come back to that.

Often the people who parade around acting the most spiritual are the least spiritual. The fruit of the Spirit isn't tongues or prophecy. The fruit is love, joy, peace, patience, kindness, self-control, and so on. Spiritual gifting *can* be evidence that the Holy Spirit is working through you, but self-control *is* evidence that the Holy Spirit is working in you. If that distinction doesn't hit you square between the eyes, it should. Think about it.

There's a direction to all this. I promise. God conversations all serve a single goal. Did you know that? Look back at the quotation from Romans at the beginning of this chapter and read it closely. The point of that passage is growth. The goal is becoming active participants of God's family more and more.

Hearing God? Those conversations are meant to *do* something. They're meant to help you grow.

Predestined to Change

As a good Father, God has a plan for you: to grow up, discover the amazing graces He's put in you, and flourish. God's plan for you is *maturity*.

The more you think about this, the more sense it will make. My parents' goal from the moment they brought us kids home from the hospital was for us to become fully functional adults with whom they could have giving, mutual, mature relationships. They were on to something. If you have kids, think about how you want them to be when they're thirty. If you don't have kids, imagine what those children could look like as young adults— best-case scenario. We're probably thinking similar thoughts. Wise. Caring. Honorable. Successful. Happy. Fun. Loving. Wealthy. Excellent. Generous. Healthy. Able to pay bills and take care of themselves and others. Knowing what they want in life and pursuing it. If we, being far from perfect, know how to give good gifts to our children, how much more does our Father in heaven want to do the same for us?

The Father is obsessed with your becoming a mature part of His family, and the Holy Spirit speaks for your spiritual formation. He is on mission from the Father, saying only what the Father tells Him to say. The role of the Holy Spirit is to bring that work of adoption to completion—not just to bring you into His family but to make you worthy of carrying His name. The truth is this: hearing God will never become part of our lives if we don't realize that His goal is to help lead us to maturity.

So can God speak to you now, while you're still growing? Yes, *now*. Even if you aren't hearing Him speak about where to find the best parking spot or who your gorgeous spouse will be or exactly what to name your baby? Yes. You don't have to feel as though you're not spiritual enough to decipher God's speech toward you. All you must do is listen and be faithful with what you *do* know.

Baby steps. Baby steps.

———

All right. Back to Romans. Let's get a little theological.

Look at the latter part of the passage from Romans 8 that opens this chapter. Basically, it's saying that our destiny is to be like Jesus, both now and to come. Let that sink in for a minute.

God's will for every Christian is to become more like Jesus *now*, so that the entire world can experience God's love. God's will is also for every Christian to become more like Jesus in the next life—like Him in His righteousness, a completed and experienced righteousness in bodily form, and to have a resurrected body like Jesus has!

Yet even now God is working on our image restoration. Man was made in the image and likeness of God, but when man fell, the image was marred. The image is still there, however, and God is restoring that image of Jesus by the work of the Holy Spirit.

Paul the apostle was a spiritual father. He saw his calling as a representative of God the Father, to father the church and treat it gently and tenderly as a father would treat his children. Paul told the Galatians that he labored in childbirth for them "until Christ is formed in you" (Galatians 4:19). He was plainly communicating the goal of his leadership in the Christian community in Galatia: the formation of little "Jesuses." In other words, *maturity*. This points back to the main point of all God's work even more. Whether directly or indirectly through His people, He is growing us into the image of Jesus.

Romans 12:2 reads, "Be transformed by the renewal of your mind, that by testing you may discern what is the will of God, what is good and acceptable and perfect." Paul is telling us the way to figure out God's will is by spiritual transformation—the renewal of our minds. Earlier we looked at that work of the Holy Spirit in the life of Jesus and at how the Holy Spirit helped Jesus come to that moment of ministry launch. Even Jesus had to grow "in wisdom and stature, and in favor with God and man" (Luke 2:52, NIV). How much more will we? We're like toddlers, and the Holy Spirit comes to mature us so we can become children of God, led by the Spirit of God into greater and greater relationship and intimacy with Him.

Growing Up

My niece Frankie is almost three. Frankie watches shows and movies like *PAW Patrol, Minions,* and *Shrek,* and then she employs the language she learns from them in her conversations. More amazing than that, those shows add little pieces to Frankie's imaginative framework—how she perceives the world. Her little brain is trying to understand the world she lives in, and those symbols and stories become maps of meaning—in other words, the basic worldview that shows her how everything fits together. (Jordan Peterson has written a wonderful book titled just that, *Maps of Meaning,* wherein he explains the concept exhaustively.[1]) Bottom line? Frankie interprets her circumstances through the narratives she knows and loves.

For example, Frankie's concept of "the beach" was given to her by *PAW Patrol.* She'd never been to the coast, but one day we overheard her saying to herself, "Frankie, do you want to go to the beach like how Marshall and Chase go to Adventure Bay?" Marshall and Chase love Adventure Bay and play around on Jet Skis. Frankie thinks good thoughts about the beach because it relates to the good thoughts she has about *PAW Patrol* characters at the beach. She even has some *PAW Patrol* water vernacular. She didn't know what a beach was, and now she does. Her mind and emotions are turned on to the idea of a beach. She fills in "beach" with the story she loves.

Now everything I say about beaches to Frankie is colored by *PAW Patrol. PAW Patrol* has given language to her, thoughts to her, ideas to her, and meaning—and with all that, it's shaped how she thinks about beaches. When I talk to Frankie about beaches, I'm not speaking into a vacuum or at a blank canvas. If I were, she wouldn't understand, because she'd have no context. As she's learned to hear words and use words and decipher what's happening in life and on television and in movies, her busy little brain is doing its best to compute what's going on in the world and trying to make sense of it.

Are we any different? Of course not. God isn't speaking into a vacuum with us. No one is a blank canvas. Our busy little brains have been gathering information about the world and its contents, false or otherwise, to make sense of it. They have created maps of meaning made of symbols and narratives, all of which help constitute our interpretive framework.

So when Paul is writing to the Romans and telling them their minds need to be changed, he's essentially saying, "The way you're thinking about this situation is inhibiting your reception of God's will." In other words, the barrier to hearing, and thus the barrier to maturity, can be what we've already "learned."

Wait, you think pensively, setting this book down for a moment. *Are you saying I might not be able to hear God because I have some ways of thinking about Him or about my situation that may block out His speech to me?*

Yeppers.

Absolutely.

If your interior map of meaning has been pieced together by a narrative that's not from God, it's *absolutely* going to block out God's speech—or at least make it dang hard to hear Him. Or if your map is about anything besides His desire for you to grow up into the loving image of Jesus, you're going to interpret things "off." Maybe not *massively* off, but on the other hand . . .

Maybe it will be off. This, when you think about it, is why people quote all the right verses for all the wrong reasons.

Expressions . . . Express?

Paul was writing to an ethnically diverse church in Rome. One group, ethnic Jews, thought Christianity could have only one cultural expression. The Roman emperors had been hostile to the Jews, particularly in Rome, and had kicked them out on several occasions. Initially the church in Rome was founded and run by Christian Jews, but when the Jews were expelled from the city, Gentiles began to run it. An emperor favorable to the Jews allowed them back into Rome, but the Jewish Christians came home to a Gentile-style church, and that felt completely foreign to them.

The Gentile Christians were eating meat that wasn't kosher. The men weren't being circumcised. All *sorts* of formal Jewish customs weren't being kept. *This is an outrage,* the Jews thought.

The church split, right down the middle. The Gentile Christians, emboldened by Paul's message of liberty in Christ Jesus, stood their ground. They didn't give in at all to the Jewish harassment regarding their diet and customs. They were free in Christ! As a result, the Jewish Christians refused to fellowship with them because they could not (for practical and ideological reasons) share the same table. If you're kosher, what do you do if every dish at the potluck has bacon in it?

Now, the Romans weren't wrong about their liberty in Christ; they were totally right. The Jews were wrong about forcing kosher law and other customs onto the Gentiles. But the Gentiles had their own issues, like a resentful attitude and some latent anti-Semitism. Both sides ended up needing to find a better way forward.

The Jewish Christians needed to read Romans 1–8 and 12–16 to understand that nobody is justified by the works of the Law and that their complaining about other people's food was making them weak in faith and unloving. The Gentiles also needed to read Romans 12–16 from the *Jews'* perspective, seeing that it would be better just to serve bread (a food everyone could eat) and leave the pork and shrimp in the back of the fridge for when Jews come over to worship at their house.

Both groups had narratives that needed help. They needed someone to give them language to help bring resolution to their problem. A modern example could be Christians who drink alcohol and Christians who do not. People need clear teaching on this issue, because in many cases it's a point of disfellowship. God's heart is unity, not separation over a drink!

Now think about this: both sides, full of the same Holy Spirit, found a way to be wrong. Paul writes the book of Romans to give them a new map of meaning, a point of reference so they can hear what God is saying to their church and find out what His desire is for them.

The truth is that God is always speaking to us, but many times we're incredibly spiritually immature. The bulk of God's communication toward us is flying right over our heads because it's for the mature, not the immature. Our maps of meaning bear about as much resemblance to what God's talking about as the coast does to computer-animated Adventure Bay.

Some of us have been Christians a long time yet remain spiritual infants. Time, alone, doesn't make us mature or like Jesus; our world is full of both young and old fools. The apostle Paul understood that when he wrote, "Among the mature we do impart wisdom" (1 Corinthians 2:6).

And the author of Hebrews wrote,

> We have much to say, and it is hard to explain, since you
> have become dull of hearing. For though by this time you
> ought to be teachers, you need someone to teach you again
> the basic principles of the oracles of God. You need milk,
> not solid food, for everyone who lives on milk is unskilled
> in the word of righteousness, since he is a child. But solid
> food is for the mature, for those who have their powers of
> discernment trained by constant practice to distinguish
> good from evil. (5:11–14)

Even though God can speak to anyone and we don't need to be perfect people to hear Him, as we grow in our spiritual maturity, we can understand His voice better.

Little Kids

This begs a sort of chicken-and-egg question. If we need maturity to hear God, but hearing Him is what helps mature us, are we stuck in a vicious circle?

Of course not. The two go hand in hand, and bit by bit God draws us into deeper understanding. Just like any learning or growing, we experience an incremental process of little advances. Sometimes that's punctuated by growth spurts, like those awkward overnight sproutings that leave teenagers tripping over their own feet. But don't become discouraged or think this process is all on you. Is growing a choice? Of course not. But what makes for healthy growth—good sleep, good nutrition, good education—involves choices.

I love new Christians. I think they're incredible. God speaks to them in miraculous, dynamic ways. I'm also extremely envious of how God tends to answer so many of their prayers in those early days, confirming His goodness and realness in a special way. (Side note: if you're a relatively new Christian, ask God for everything now!)

But let's face it. New Christians also say the most off-the-wall stuff, a little like my niece Frankie. Why? Because they're spiritual toddlers. Their maps of meaning are infantile. Their worldview is often informed by assumptions, untested opinions, or the theological equivalents of *Shrek, Minions,* and *PAW Patrol.*

Frankie is learning the ABCs of existence. We aren't talking about what she's going to do for her sixteenth birthday or what kind of job she wants or whom she wants to marry. An order of priorities in our speech toward Frankie has been determined by the people who know what's best for her. Frankie often tires of her *Groundhog Day* life—the same things seem to happen over and over. But consistency over time is building an interpretive framework in Frankie that's going to help her navigate through life with a confidence and ease that's second nature.

It's not first nature for Frankie to be responsible. And she's not a Vos yet (Vos is her father's surname). Voses don't throw their breakfast on the floor. Voses don't hit Mummy or Grandma in the face when they're mad. Voses don't cry before they go to bed. Voses don't complain and disobey every time they're asked to clean up a mess they made. Voses don't venture out onto the road without looking both ways. Voses don't take off all their clothes in public and run around naked. Frankie is at once *completely* a Vos and yet *still becoming* a Vos. The process of Frankie becoming a Vos is shaped by what she hears and must respond to. It's also shaped by people who enforce the family values in her life (Mum and Dad, Grandma and Grandpa, Uncle Nate, her babysitters).

It's important to know where we are in our walk when we're trying to decipher God's voice. It helps us not to get frustrated but to focus on becoming what we're supposed to become. But how do we know where we are? Well, it starts by trying to clearly see the real state of what has shaped our capacity to listen.

You see, most of us don't want to admit that our maps of meaning are off. We couldn't *possibly* have some malformed assumptions. Our political view is *obviously* perfect and informed. Our stance on contentious issues? *Unassailable.* Our knowledge and feelings about the world? Life? Relationships? *A vision of perfection, dahling.*

But when we can't question our assumptions, how can we have a place to begin listening? So we exchange what's real for what's comfortable. We settle for pop psychology and what feels good instead of biblical patterns of formation.

Real spiritual growth feels about as fun as being a kid with parents telling you what to do. It feels like growing pains. Why? Because spiritual formation doesn't happen outside the context of real relationship. And that's hard.

Restoring the Image

Frankie is becoming a Vos so she can do Vos stuff. God is restoring the image of God so you can be part of the family, have the family name, and do things the way the family does them. He wants you to partake of the divine nature so you can partake of the divine function. He wants you to rule and reign in life. But you must learn how to do that, so He's going to talk to you a lot about that!

You are saved by grace for works so you can grow into the image of Jesus. Philippians 3:12 reads, "I press on, that I may lay hold of that for which Christ Jesus has also laid hold of me" (NKJV).

Jesus laid hold of you for a reason. Salvation isn't catch and release. God doesn't save you and then turn you loose into a better river solely dedicated to your eternal, cushy comfort. He saves you for His purposes—you have a job to do! Ephesians 2:10 reads, "We are his workmanship, created in Christ Jesus for good works, which God prepared beforehand, that we should walk in them." You were created for good works. That's why you were saved and re-created in Christ Jesus. The image of Christ is restored so you can be part of the family and do the family stuff!

Don't resist God. Don't pull a Frankie and cry and whine and embarrass yourself. Take God's discipline and keep moving. *Boom.* The focus of God's Fatherhood is on this very issue: training you up in the way you should go. This is what He is passionate about! This is what He is speaking to.

And if He loves you, He will put people in your life who will speak this training and discipline into your life. He will be vocal toward you for your growth.

As we are learning what to do, we're learning our language as well. The relationship and the function are interdependent and overlap, weaving together and growing together.

Hebrews 12:11 says, "For the moment all discipline seems painful rather than pleasant, but later it yields the peaceful fruit of righteousness to those who have been trained by it."

If God spoke only to superspiritual people, He'd never speak. God isn't Regina George from the movie *Mean Girls* at a high school party, talking only to people from the in-crowd. But with that said, growing in the Holy Spirit does require action on our part. We can listen, and we can respond.

I've always struggled to speak well of my mistakes and the way I've been disciplined by God. Honestly, I've tended to resent the people God has used to mature me. But now I find that I'm becoming that person myself. Having learned the language and in many ways become the language used to shape me, I'm now using that language to shape others. And that language is used in how I understand God and represent Him to others as they mature.

The grace of God that trains us and brings the peaceful fruit of righteousness is by no means always enjoyable. *Nathan,* I ask myself, *did you think God's speech toward you would always be soft whispers in your ear? Was your map of meaning limited to your sitting down with a mug of coffee in your "quiet place," all curled up in front of a fire with your blankie and some worship music in the background?*

Hahahahahahaha.

God's voice can be your boss telling you he's writing you up because you're late for the third time. God's voice can be that high school teacher who's caught you cheating (and by the way, you've failed the class). God's voice can be the police officer who's pulled you over for speeding. God's voice can be the woman behind you who points out that you just butted in line. God's voice can be your mom telling you to clean your room. God's voice can be your brother telling you to chill out. God's voice can be your paper getting a C minus because you didn't try hard enough. God's voice can be you not getting the promotion because, frankly, you haven't put in the work.

LeBron James wasn't born with a basketball in his hand. His ability on the court isn't first nature; it's second nature. When LeBron plays basketball, it looks like it's all natural to him, but it isn't. His first nature is not to understand anything that comes out of the coach's mouth. His first nature is to miss baskets. His second nature, however, is the result of process and practice. He's become so familiar with the game of basketball that he can understand all the plays, strategies, positions, and calls. He can hear a call from the court and then put that call into action. It's all become second nature.

God wants strong sons and daughters, with this "second nature" in full swing. He wants sons and daughters of character. He wants sons and daughters with whom He can have a "real talk" relationship. Yeah, He loves you as an infant and will always bless you and think good thoughts about you that way. But as a Father, He wants maturity for you, and He wants to get you there sooner rather than later. He's going to be talking about that right now and talking about it a lot. He wants you to understand His will. He doesn't need you to be perfect to understand it, but He needs your mind and heart to be renovated by the processes and practices that will bring about a trained and matured man or woman of God.

How is God growing you? Think about some areas that you've struggled in but are learning from. Can you see the value in the lessons yet? Or are they just painful to remember? Growth can be embarrassing, but if it's real, we've heard something from God.

One day, by the grace of God at work in us, those impossible "jump shots" will seem like second nature. People won't have seen the lifetime of misses and the countless hours of submitting to the work of God in our lives. They'll see the fruit of a processed and practiced life—a son or daughter coming into the family business of abundant and victorious life.

 Remember: God speaks for our growth. We need to surrender to His process of maturity and let Him talk on His own terms.

CHAPTER THREE

The Myth of Hunky-Dory La-La Land

Why Can't Everybody Just Quiet Down Already? I'm Trying to Listen Here!

I waited patiently for the LORD;

    he inclined to me and heard my cry.

[He drew me up from the noisy pit—the tumultuous

      waters of the underworld—the mud of the swamp,]

and set my feet upon a rock,

    making my steps secure.

He put a new song in my mouth,

    a song of praise to our God.

Many will see and fear,

    and put their trust in the LORD.

—PSALM 40:1–3, AUTHOR'S PARAPHRASE ENCLOSED IN BRACKETS

I spent three years living in the East Village of New York City, which sometimes seems like a sort of urban dormitory hosting university students, artists, musicians, young professionals, and hipsters of every persuasion. Think cheap eats, expensive coffee, dive bars, and psychics. *Lots* of psychics.

Let's consider the economics of this plethora of psychics for a moment. Ladies and gentlemen, these people own storefront property in *New York Freakin' City*! What does that mean? People are *coming*. People are *paying*. They're swiping their credit cards en masse for the promise of spiritual guidance—never mind that the crystal ball advertised is neon, or that if the people were truly psychic, one would think they'd win the Mega Millions lottery a few times and go off to build a Doctor Strange–style voodoo mansion in Malibu or something.

But let's be honest. Storefront psychics aren't there because of their moral goodness or the reality of a gift (at least not in my estimation). They're there because people are desperate.

These crystal ball readers know something: Deep down, people feel spiritually bankrupt and morally confused, and their internal compasses are spinning in circles. They don't know what to do or where to turn, and they're willing to pay good money to find some sort of shadowy purpose. They're willing to use their Visas to grasp at some kind of life preserver for their sense of meaning. They're desperate to be pointed in the right direction by someone— *anyone*—who seems to have an "in" on the "other side," even if that someone might be pretending. The world they live in is so confusing, so disjointed, so *noisy,* that they'll turn to anything for clarity. Why? The distraction. *The distraction.* Anything feels better than the distraction.

Let's be honest again. We all know exactly what that feels like.

Distracti— Wait, What?

We've talked about what hearing God means (a conversation as part of a relationship) and why He speaks to us (to grow us into the image of Jesus). But now we need to turn to the elephant in the room. God's not the only one speaking. A myth floating around says this world is somehow all fine and hunky-dory la-la land, free of opposition or danger. Or it's so messed up that we have no hope of hearing God. Both ideas are, of course, wrong. But the danger of distraction is so real, and if we don't deal with it, we'll never hear God with faithful confidence.

Have you ever tried to follow a conversation while someone nearby is talking about something interesting? You find your brain constantly popping back and forth between the conversations, not exactly present in either. Now up that dynamic a hundredfold and you're getting close to the difficulty of hearing God in a noisy and distracted world.

It's easy for us to think this is a modern phenomenon—and for sure, we're tech idiots these days, obsessed with bringing the noise nonstop right into our heads and hearts with those blasted little screens we carry around. But this problem has always been there, no matter how checked out of culture Christians have become—like how *desert monks* talk about struggling with distraction.

But we're still faced with a dilemma: What do we do when we're trying to hear God in a culture of noise? Can you hear a whisper when the whole world is yelling around you?

To answer that, let's talk about superstition. And to talk about that, let's talk about Halloween. And to talk about that, let's talk about my parents.

They were first-generation Christians, with plenty of fresh memories about life in "the world." As a result (and I sympathize with them) they were especially strict. They didn't want the world to screw up us kids the way the world, they said, "screwed us up." So they did all they could for cultural noise reduction, probably more than they needed to. I mean, we didn't even have a *television* for most of my childhood.

So Halloween—that pagan holiday when Satan cavorts through suburbia, luring children with Tootsie Rolls? Ha! Forget about it. My parents shut off the lights throughout the entire house that night and pretended we weren't home. For real. Just so we wouldn't have to deal with awkward trick-or-treating encounters, kids ringing the doorbell only for us to have to explain . . . what? That they were *serving Satan* with their *costumed candy coveting*?

Our church offered a "Hallelujah" party (an alternative to Halloween), where kids were encouraged to dress up in "wholesome" costumes (that's Christianese for "Bible characters"), but the payout at the end of the night was always ludicrous: we'd get one miserable bag of candy, knowing that everyone else was doing Scrooge McDuck dives into their mounds of candy plunder. It was maddening. My brother and I protested, calling the party a "rip-off." So my dad changed the game: the next Halloween he took us to play pool and see a movie. That was a massive sacrifice for my parents, because they didn't have much money.

But, oh, that next morning . . . Some of our friends at the tiny private Christian school we attended would show up on November 1 with sugary treasures galore from the raid they'd made on the enemy camp the night before. Debates about the morality of trick-or-treating ensued, of course, with trenchant philosophical soliloquies preponderating. My dad always responded with, "I don't care if the Hamiltons jump off a bridge into a lake! *As for me and my house* . . . "

They were doing their best as parents. They had pure motivations. Then time did its work. They lightened up massively toward the end of our teens. Finally, my dad let us run around the neighborhood and get candy when I was about fourteen. But it was too late for us to enjoy the costumes and fun as kids.

Looking back, their response was not that of the reasoned or mature believer. It was a superstitious response. Just like people shudder at the thought of walking under a ladder or a black cat crossing their path, "touching" Halloween was, to my parents, forbidden. Taboo. Dangerous. They were scared that Halloween and all its dark themes would corrupt their kids, and they weren't willing to take that risk.

See, here's the thing: people, Christian and not, are superstitious. At its root, superstition is introducing a competing voice that threatens to distract us from God's voice—*even if that competing voice is trying to get rid of other voices.* No matter who we are, we can struggle with this kind of superstitious thinking. The way you know something is a "superstition" is that there's no clear logic for it, yet you worry like crazy about what will happen if you engage in or encounter that something.

Let's try to sort this out as unsuperstitiously as possible. (Yeah, you with the dictionary! *Unsuperstitiously* is a word. As of right now.) We'll start with just trying to see what we're dealing with. To use the Bible's categories, three major voices are competing with God's voice: the "world," the "flesh," and the "devil." Each of these voices represents a whole category of distraction we deal with. Each of them contributes to making it difficult to hear God clearly, like trying to follow a quiet conversation in Times Square. Why is it so hard? *The noise.*

Let's look at each of these avenues of noise and distraction in turn. (We'll take them slightly out of order, though, to circle from furthest away from us to the most intimate: devil, world, then flesh.)

The Devil (or El Diablo)

Yes, I am one of those old-fashioned people who believes in the devil. But not like the *Far Side* cartoon devil. And not like the come-outta-him-spirit-of-wickedness specter that big-hair tel-evangelists seem to talk about a lot. I don't blame him for very many of my day-to-day woes. I don't think he's capable of half the stuff we superstitiously give him credit for. I usually tell my students that the devil probably doesn't even know their names.

You see, the devil is not omnipotent—he doesn't have power over all or power over God's angels. The devil is not omnipresent—he's not everywhere at once, and he's limited to his being. The devil is not omniscient—he's not all-knowing or knowing everything. He can't read your mind or thoughts. He's not sitting there waiting for you to say something bad and then work you over because of your bad confession. Not every Christian is under demonic attack. Satan is not creeping through your windows at night. Your wild, superstitious, faith-lacking imagination is doing that for him. People who lack faith play right into his hands. I think this is why John called the Judaizers members of "the synagogue of Satan" (Revelation 3:9). I think they were doing the devil's job by putting all kinds of ridiculous fear into Gentile hearts that didn't need to be there.

But in some ways, that quiet action is just as destructive.

The devil is a spiritual being who hates God and goodness. He works strategically; he's working to corrupt the world and frame its systems to maximize the most damage. Sure, he wants to destroy lives and snuff out the candle of human potential, but probably more important, he's sticking to his main and master plan: to distort and twist God's voice so we no longer know which way is up, and even the neon storefront lights that blink out "Psychic Readings" start to look appealing.

Let's go back to Genesis 3. From the beginning, the devil's strategy was to mess up people by wedging himself between them and God's words.

The first thing the serpent did was question the word: "Did God really say . . . ?" Think about that. His first move was to cause doubt and confusion about God's *speech*. The devil messed with Eve when she was alone and at her most vulnerable. He did the same with Jesus, and when he left Jesus, Scripture says he would return at "an opportune time" (Luke 4:13).

Now, Jesus is the clearest speech we have ever heard from the Father. Jesus is the Logos (that's Greek for "the Word," but, like, with a capital *W*). The Word became flesh and dwelt among us! The devil is always trying to bring Jesus down. He attacks the Logos. It's an old trick, but it's the devil's best one.

To paraphrase, the serpent in the garden said, "Are you sure God didn't mean something else? It's okay. It's perfectly normal to question what God said." Or how about this?: "Perhaps you heard Him wrong! Yeah, maybe God didn't mean it *that* way but meant it *this* way!"

After he questioned the word, Eve felt comfortable "adding to" it: "God said we must not eat the fruit, *nor even touch it,* lest we die."

God didn't say not to *touch* the fruit; He said not to *eat* it. The human error of adding to God's Word isn't because we can't have any good ideas ourselves; it's about our tendency to spin—to make God's utterance seem harsh or unreasonable (according to our own reasoning), especially impossible to ourselves. We "rational-ize" God's words in ways that rarely make things easier on us, adding to what He has said, as if our unreasonable and super-stitious natures were His own.

Our tendency is to view God's call as impossible, especially when it seems inconsistent with what we see. But Eve's question-ing and adding to God's word made the devil's obvious lie some-how more palatable. He'd twisted the word. He rarely fully lies; he just tells half-truths, which are somehow twice as convincing, yet as wrong as a lie of the purest kind.

When Jesus was in the wilderness, fasting for forty days, the devil came along to tempt Him. (He was alone and hungry, and probably more than a little hangry.) How did he tempt Jesus? Not by quoting some black magic necromantic occult tome or some-thing but by using the *Bible*.

Stop right there.

The devil used the *Bible* to tempt Jesus. In other words, he tried to use God's own words against Him! Remember his first trick in the garden? He used his best trick against Jesus too! He twisted God's words to try to get Jesus to do what Eve did—to become self-sufficient, falsely independent. He took God's words out of context to suit his purposes.

Again, the Finochio Amplified Version says,

Take this stone and make it bread! Take this fruit and eat of it. Be like God and have your own bread! Don't be dependent! Find your own way for your life. Don't inquire of the Lord and wait for His voice and timing; get a word from the Lord now through this easier and more conve-nient way!

What did Jesus do in response? He quoted Scripture in its proper context. He used God's words, not His own words, to fight the devil.

Satan's big plan of attack against God's people is always *confusion.* He wants to twist and distort God's voice so that we find ourselves as alienated and alone as he is. He wants us to be distracted like he's distracted, to make others suffer like he does, in a world full of noise, void of the voices of hope, peace, and clarity. He's willing to do anything to keep us from hearing God.

The World

Today, the words of Jesus are being twisted and corrupted more than ever. And increasingly, the world context we find ourselves in tries to distract Christians by means of "Jesus-and." Often, syncretism (mixing and diluting beliefs) is more effective than opposition. This voice often says all kinds of soothing, tempting things: *Have a little Jesus; He's into peace and love! He's so serving and forgiving! Sit down and have a pedicure; allow Jesus to massage those tired little feet of yours. You don't need to listen to anything else He had to say except, "I have come that they may have life, and life to the full!"* Is anything more distracting than comfort? We want to listen to this, because it lulls us away from the core realities of following Jesus: that there are real and often painful sacrifices to be made in service of growth and life. The world hardly ever tries to take away your cake. It tries to convince you that you can have it and eat it too.

Each society interprets this in its own way. For example,

Rome was a syncretistic society, pressuring Christians to blend
Jesus with various diluting influences. You know, little teensy
tiny things, like *worshipping the emperor.* Everyone could be
spiritual and religious as long as they didn't believe the exclusive
words of Jesus. Today, it's a bit quieter but still so pernicious. *Go
to church on Sunday and have fun, but don't read the gospel of
John, whatever you do. Don't challenge the status quo. Be comfortable. Got it?*

Just as the devil attacks God's words as part of his major business, he works to create a world system hostile to God's Word.
Then he doesn't have to do the hard stuff. And just like with the
temptation of Jesus, some of his most effective attacks come
clothed in good and half-truth.

Take religion, for example. Humanity is obsessed with religion (which, to be honest, is often just mainstream superstition).
We aren't the way we should be, the world is wrong, we're aware
of it, and so we're trying to bring ourselves up. That's what religions always do, remember? They try to bring humanity up closer
to God's level, though the gospel says God has already come down
to ours. Christianity is markedly different in that it lowers man—it
shows us the very depths of our depravity, and then it brings Jesus
to us. Religion tries to bring man up to God. Jesus brought the
Father down to us, where we are. We've even turned the teachings
of Jesus into a religion just as much as any other. If you think the
devil can't use Christianity for his own purposes, then you haven't
been paying much attention.

All these religions that we've created are essentially maps of
meaning: ways we're trying to navigate this broken and fallen

world. Our religions are patterns that give symbols and meaning to life while we're here, but we think that's all they are.

In our current materialistic society, we think that matter is all that's real and that no shaping or guiding spiritual forces are at work. But that's not the case. Our religion of power says work gives life meaning. Our religion of sex says sexual expression and prowess and erotic love fulfill us and give life meaning. Our religion of academia tells us being smart and knowing a lot give life meaning. These are all just symbols and patterns not from God; they're distortions of things God created. False religions create a competing set of meanings that distract from God's voice by being so close to it. Other physical joys distract us by reinforcing the lie that the highest human experience is physical pleasure. Ultimately, they add up to the same thing: noise.

Noise.

Noise.

The Flesh

Our flesh is the third massive competing voice vying to steal our attention from God.

The flesh is an unredeemed inner will and desire, which must be worked out slowly as we mature in Jesus. Typically that unredeemed will and desire are in constant competition with God's will and desire, the same way a bratty toddler's will (to eat nothing but candy, never sleep, and watch Netflix all day) conflicts with a responsible parent. The devil and the world don't have to do all that much to make us sin and veer off course. We're self-deceived by our own desires, and we easily confuse our own voice for God's! How stupid is that? But every one of us does it.

Between the flesh and the world system he's built, the devil can pretty much sit back, relax, and watch us shoot ourselves in the feet—constantly! Most of my mistakes aren't even the world telling me what I want and don't want. *I'm* the problem. It's a mistake to always pin the blame for my distraction on things outside me.

Paul doesn't teach us to crucify the world with its passions; he tells us to crucify the *flesh* with its passions (Galatians 5:24). I don't need slick advertisements about ice cream to want to eat, like, a *thousand* gelatos. I've figured out that I like to do that all on my own! My flesh is lazy. My flesh is unwilling. It's a tyrant. It's never satisfied and always complaining about God and life and everyone else.

Every day I must nail it to the cross. The dang thing won't up'n stay crucified, which is the most annoying part. I get so tired of having to nail Nathan and all his wild desires to the cross. It's infuriating. Every day I wake up, and I'm, like, "You again! I thought you were dead! I thought we dealt with this yesterday!"

Not much more I can say on this one, right? If you're human, you know what I'm talking about.

(And if you're not human, how are you reading this book?)

Above the Noise

We see that the world, the flesh, and the devil are all working in an unholy trio of three evil stooges to create a ton of noise. They're working in a demonic choreography to confuse what God says. It's a mess.

They're all in play for each of us, but some of us struggle more than others with issues of noise and distraction. All Christians have a voice they turn to when the going gets tough and it seems as though God's not saying anything. (Just like King Saul did, visiting the medium of En-dor—1 Samuel 28.) Maybe it's not a New York psychic or superstitions about Halloween for you. Maybe it's the stock market. Maybe it's Instagram. Maybe it's political pundits. Maybe it's your weirdly reassuring aunt Edwina.

We all appeal for direction to realities that seem to comfort us with their illusion of security. We often consult these securities as if they're speaking on behalf of heaven. In Matthew 16:22, Peter tries to dissuade Jesus from doing something foolish to jeopardize His life, speaking from a sense of security. All Peter was doing was trying to protect his rabbi and friend, but Jesus rebuked Peter and said, "Get behind me, Satan! You are a hindrance to me. For you are not setting your mind on the things of God, but on the things of man" (verse 23). Think of that! Jesus interpreted even His close friend's words as those of the devil. Why? *Because they were a distraction.* The path they hinted at was one of comfort, not the way of the cross.

Between the world and our flesh and the devil and his demons, we hear a lot of noise. I think noise is the biggest dilemma we face: all the voices in our lives, the nonstop lifestyle advertising, everyone else's ambitions, what the world tells us about happiness, what our flesh is telling us will make us happy, the temptations the devil and his demons have created to try to persuade us to consult clearly ungodly voices. Noise is Satan's specialty. Our world isn't getting quieter; consider the advent of those noise machines we carry around in our hands.

The Miry Clay

I love Psalm 40 and the Hebrew language used in this passage. The Hebrews thought of the underworld as a watery, dark, noisy place, and some Bible translations use the words "miry clay" or "miry bog." Regardless, the idea is pandemonium and confusion: an inability to rest one's thoughts because of the loop of chaos cycling through.

Have you ever felt like your world is pure noise? I think those of us who deal with anxiety feel that way at times. It's as if the world externally and our world internally are both turned up to a ten. I wonder if the psalmist here is dealing with some serious anxiety about a situation that's stressing him out. The external situation is driving him nuts, and internally he's losing it. What does he do? He waits for the Lord.

This is the path forward for us too. *Waiting*. Letting things settle. David creates some space, and he must wait "patiently" for God. He could easily consult something or someone else. He could appeal to a more convenient voice—one that could answer him quicker. But he decides to wait patiently. His flesh is going to have to learn patience. The world can wait. David's mortal enemies can chill out for a while. David has decided to wait patiently for the Lord.

You see, one of the greatest threats to the world, flesh, and devil is simple—patience. Stopping. Hell hates someone brave enough to quiet down when life gets noisy.

David knows where his help comes from. Not from other people, not from his own strength or ingenuity, but from God. David has closed his laptop; he's not googling to get answers; he's not going to the medium Saul consulted; he's not counsel searching his advisers, looking for the answer he wants to hear. He's slowed down time, gone to his secret place. Maybe he picks up his harp. Maybe he takes a walk. In any case, he's *listening*. He can't make God speak, but he can try to be ready for when He does.

Waiting for God means allowing space for God to speak. Waiting for God involves God-centered activities, being in the places where He can be found and being found in the places He's called us to work. Perhaps God's voice came to David in a worship service in the tabernacle while the choir was singing, the musicians were playing, and the congregation was rejoicing. Perhaps God's voice came as David read Miriam's prophetic song of God's deliverance that she sang on the shores of the Red Sea. Perhaps God's voice came as he was present with his family and children. Perhaps God's voice came as his attitude began to change from the inside out, as he started to trust that God was going to take care of everything and that he didn't need to carry this weight. Perhaps God's voice came as he wrote songs deep into the night with his scribe.

And God delivers.

Many times, actively waiting for God is an intentional breaking from striving. It's not quitting your job but rather quitting your conniving, strategizing, networking, overworking plans to try to do everything yourself, and a coming to terms with the fact that God is God and has better ways of doing things. Do a word search on *inquire* in the Old Testament. The kings who inquired of the Lord got a strategic word from God, and the kings who failed to inquire of the Lord ended up making some boneheaded decisions.

This doesn't mean that we don't get wisdom from other people, or that we don't read books about our situation, or that we give up or stop digging. It means we decide to acknowledge God's sovereignty—His good rule and reign over our lives—and His desire and ability to work on our behalf. Waiting for the Lord overcomes our worry and superstition.

Many of us are totally cynical about God. We've had experiences that tend to dictate to our souls how we think and feel about Him rather than allowing His revelation of Himself to dictate how we ought to think and feel about Him. The world, the flesh, and the devil don't want you to think of God as Forgiver, Healer, or someone who's redeeming your life from the miry clay! The world, the flesh, and the devil always have the bad news. God always has the good news.

Every time we appeal to a god or religious system or spiritual guidance (from street-corner psychics to conservative Halloween taboos) that is not from the good God of the Bible, we're opening ourselves to words that are simply going to be too small, too cynical, and too short of what God has in store for us.

To paraphrase G. K. Chesterton, the world has grown old, but God has stayed young.[2] God has words that will keep you young and childlike, believing and hoping the best. Your cynical, old, corrupt mind and the world around you will give you only the same cynical, terrified guidance that tries to steer you toward illusions of safety.

God is your rock, your fortress, and your deliverer! He's your safety, and He is your God! Choose to wait for Him, for His words, and decide to actively engage in the waiting-for-God processes of church, community, devotion, Scripture reading, prayer, fasting, generosity, and faithfulness.

In that waiting you might find that the noise begins to drop. That distractions wither. That superstitions begin to look as hollow as neon lights. And that the voice you've been trying to hear suddenly becomes clear.

That's what I'm beginning to learn. And it's so worth it.

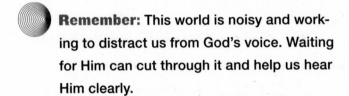

Remember: This world is noisy and working to distract us from God's voice. Waiting for Him can cut through it and help us hear Him clearly.

CHAPTER FOUR

The Myth of the Easy Book

Praise God for the Bible! Now, If We Just Knew How to Read It

All Scripture is God-breathed and is useful for teaching, rebuking, correcting and training in righteousness.

—2 TIMOTHY 3:16, NIV

I read *Macbeth* in eleventh grade. It was great, except for one minor detail: I had no idea what the heck was going on. I could guess from the action sequences what was transpiring, but the dialogue may as well have been written in Chinese. It felt so foreign.

Now, I was used to old books. I was a private-school bookworm who tested high for reading comprehension. My parents were broke when we were kids, so we used to go to the local library all the time for free movies and books. In the throes of desperation, I voluntarily read T. E. Lawrence's *Seven Pillars of Wisdom* and Tolstoy's *War and Peace* as an eleven-year-old. All that to say, I could get jiggy with a few "thees" and "thous," maybe even the odd "prithee." But even as an English nerd, I couldn't understand Shakespeare.

That didn't mean it wasn't beautiful.

That didn't mean it wasn't brilliant.

It just meant I *couldn't*.

Revise that. It wasn't that I couldn't; I just needed help.

I needed a guide, that was the thing. I needed someone to explain unfamiliar terms and phrases, someone to point out when a metaphor was metaphor-ing and precisely when those pesky iambs were pentameter-ing. I was so frustrated at my lack of ability to interpret *Macbeth* that I obstinately dug in. Sure, it was hard, but I trusted that it would be worth it. That made me grit my teeth. I would get this. I *would*.

Desperate for clues, I watched an old *Macbeth* movie. And I saw it performed by a prominent Shakespearean company. I even memorized Lady Macbeth's dagger soliloquy (*"Come, you spirits that tend on mortal thoughts"*).[3]

In my crowning act of literary despondency, I even bought a commentary by a Shakespearean scholar. But even with all this, I felt stuck. Shakespeare felt like a foreign language that had to be learned, a strange culture one must live in to "get" it.

When I went to see the actual play, sitting behind an elderly man and woman who kept kept *laughing* at different lines, I could hardly even make out what was being said, let alone understand them, let alone *get the joke.* Have you ever met someone with a vastly different accent from yours? To the point that even though you both spoke the same language, you found yourself unable to understand, like, every other word? You sort of stood there like an idiot, nodding and smiling, laughing when they laughed, grasping at anything familiar so you could chip in and feel connected? That was me at the *Macbeth* play. A masterpiece was whizzing over my head. But I was looking around, all *Isn't this a great breeze, guys? Gotta* love *these frisky Shakespearean breezes.*

The elderly couple in front of me were having the time of their lives. I could tell this wasn't their first rodeo. Maybe they'd been to Stratford before and were probably experts or at least lifelong fans. They'd read the plays, the commentaries, the program, and they knew all the actors. They probably knew the histories behind the plays—when they were written, who they were written for, and what sort of hot water Shakespeare got into when he put on the plays in Merry Olde England.

What kind of person laughs at all the "inside" Shakespeare jokes while everyone else in the crowd is totally befuddled? Shakespeare jokes don't come easy. That's some highbrow stuff. For us today—centuries after he wrote—Shakespeare's work isn't "pop" English. He wrote in a language that now often sounds foreign, to a crowd with unique circumstances, about complex life issues, and with a wit and precision that are otherworldly.

But learning to understand ideas and language different from our own is *worth* it. Our view of the world is expanded by encountering those ideas and languages. They're hard because they're different, but they're *valuable* for the same reason. After all, if Shakespeare had written the way we talk, would we still be reading his words today? Probably not. Encountering great literature gives us a way to view the world that connects us to the author *and* to the author's audiences throughout history.

That's just as true of the Bible as it is of *Macbeth*. So why do we give up on God's book so easily—or just plain read it *wrong*?

The Beautiful, Difficult Book

I wrote this section on an airplane on my way back from England, where my wife and I had just spent the last week visiting the graves of all our literary heroes. During the trip we watched a British

television series about Thomas Cromwell called *Wolf Hall.*
Throughout the series we saw the birth pains of the Protestant
Reformation in England, which ultimately came down to what
people thought should be done with the Bible. Some people believed the Bible should be translated into the common language so
that the common people could read the Bible for themselves. That
thought was so threatening to the institutional church (whose interpretation and control of faith bore immense political power)
that it carried a literal death sentence for many.

I learned all about them from *Fox's Book of Martyrs,*[4] a book
about men and women who were tortured and burned at the stake
for printing and distributing English Bibles. The access we have to
the Bible today, and our rich tradition of valuing our own copies
of it, is possible because of these people, and we owe it to them to
read it and preach it and teach it and treasure it. At the same time,
I can't help but think about all the people who died because of
misrepresentations and poor interpretations of this book.

Because the other shoe—the implications of everyone, their
mother, and their duck owning a Bible—has surely dropped. No
longer do you have to pass even a flawed priestly exam or ordina-
tion to teach from it. On one side we have political suppression of
the book—the Catholic Church insisting that the book must be
interpreted by the church alone and not by common people. On
the other side we have our current state of free-for-all, a Wild West
of interpretation. That fenceless wilderness has given birth to everything from death cults to the "Christian Blogosphere."

Most of us obviously live somewhere in the middle. We trust
certain people to interpret the Bible for us. We're confident about

certain opinions and doubtful about others. But if God is speaking through this strange, wonderful book, how do we know we're getting His true meaning? (Scripture *does* have correct interpretations; they absolutely do exist. Denying this is playing into the gibberish of postmodernism. You know, that this-is-what-it-means-to-me jargon.)

Who cares what *Macbeth* means to you? What did it mean to the original audience? What did Shakespeare *intend* it to mean? Let's start there! You aren't the center of the universe. You didn't write *Macbeth;* somebody else did. As much as it's great to share your opinion, if there's no evidence for what you believe in the text, then you're out of line, in danger of using the play just to bolster what you already know. When it comes to the Bible, if that's your approach, you *can't* hear God through it, and you *can't* grow. Why? *Because you aren't letting the book be different from you.* If you make it only all about you, how in the world are you ever going to be challenged enough to grow?

Culture has failed us here. People in my generation think everything is about them. (I suspect we aren't the only ones, but we have it bad.) We're totally confused about the Bible because we're totally confused about the nature of reality. The modern sentiment, having its roots in Hume from the eighteenth century, has been that objectivity is impossible, and therefore no objectivity is possible.[5] That's not as much an intellectual belief as much as it's a general feeling. We get squirmy when someone says confidently (about anything), "This is what it means." We would rather wallow in tepid, relativistic doubt than plant a flag in something worth our conviction.

In this age we walk on eggshells around one another, hoping

not to give off airs of confidence or, God forbid, *conclusions*. Have you ever noticed that everything these days is about a conversation but never about a conclusion? Why? Because people's feelings get hurt when you disagree with them! Yikes!

"Well, that's just your opinion," we fire back at the few who do take a stand, as if that makes any sense. I don't "just" have opinions. I don't say things I don't believe, and you don't say things you don't believe. If I didn't think it was true, I wouldn't call it my opinion. An opinion is somebody's truth statement.

Now—tough question: How do you think this culture has trained you to view the Scriptures? If I can get uncomfortable for a moment, let me tell you my best guess.

As a highly self-centric (self-discovering, self-authoring, self-aggrandizing, self-realizing) child of the posttruth age, your entire interpretive framework (that has been constructed throughout school and university and by movies and Netflix and your personal trainer and the dude at the fancy grocery story that helps you find the plant-based protein snacks telling you how he voted and why) probably needs to be deconstructed and then reconstructed if you want to hear God the clearest you've ever heard Him.

I know my view has certainly been smashed to bits and put back together.

You see, most of my life I read the Bible without necessarily understanding what it meant. That's frustrating because you can almost never put your finger on what's wrong. You know most of the words, like you know Shakespeare's, *but you feel like you're missing the point.* I think most of my Bible reading was "instinctual," in the sense of *Whatever I think this means must be what it means.* In other words, I had unlearning to do before I could get down with what God was trying to say.

To a degree, we can't cheat our way through this sort of awkward growing phase of Bible reading. We all must get familiar with the text, and there's no way around that. It's sort of like watching your favorite television show the first time through. I didn't get all the richness of *The Office* until about the fifth time through. It just keeps getting better and better. But even that analogy breaks down because it assumes we know what's going on in the Bible's text, and that the more we read it, the more we'll understand it.

The greatest breakthrough I ever had was when I began asking my dad a bunch of questions about the Bible. The second greatest breakthrough was having an argumentative youth pastor, fresh out of Bible college, who I could ask my *other* questions. But the learning hasn't stopped. Breakthroughs in understanding still come. I'm still growing. I'm still a student.

Understanding the Bible ends when you think you're not a student anymore—when you've stopped asking questions of the text and others. You don't need a seminary degree to find the right interpretation of Scripture; you just need a humble and hungry heart that's willing to ask questions from anyone who knows more than you do. The greatest scholars never graduate from asking questions like "What did this mean to the author, and what did this mean to the original audience?" They never stop asking questions of others who have already studied the material.

A good theologian is just someone who's asked more questions than you have. Better yet, who's started asking the *right* questions. Connecting with the questions others have asked can help us answer our own.

Maybe that elderly couple watching *Macbeth* can explain what we're seeing?

Four Statements About the Bible

Let me testify clearly that the Bible is worth all the effort. God has spoken in this book in a way that is difficult, historic, beautiful, and totally unique. A uniting, comforting power in the Bible's presence helps us ground our thoughts and theology, getting (literally) on the same page as millions of other believers throughout the centuries. That's special. No other Christian experience does that with the same depth or consistency.

Let's look at four statements about this miraculous book that can help give us new lenses to read it—and allow our lives to be changed as we hear God through it. So much richness and life are waiting for us behind the confusion. Or maybe waiting to find us. These principles aren't the only things to keep in mind, but they're the place to begin shifting our way of reading to one that helps us hear God better in His book.

First, *the Bible is God's Word, not man's word.* Second Timothy 3:16 says, "All Scripture is God-breathed" (NIV). All of it. God *breathed* all of it. It has more authority on who God is and how to be a human than any other book written, because God Himself breathed it out onto its pages. The Bible isn't a man-made book. It isn't man's opinion on morality or how man perceives God. It's God's opinion on morality and what He's telling us about Himself. A book like this, then, has a great deal of value for anybody who wants to know about God (His self-revelation) and about humanity (God telling humanity, which He created, what it was created for).

Therefore, when you're reading the Bible, you shouldn't be reading it the same way you would read any other book. You use the same skills, of course, but you also must recognize the Bible has a spiritual life and a dimension to the text that are different. This is what we mean by the doctrine of inspiration: even though men wrote the Bible, it was *inspired* by the Holy Spirit, and the words in it are, for lack of a better image, "God-breathed" words. If that's true, and I believe it is, then that fact starts to confirm our need to get beyond impressionistic, me-first readings.

Second, *the Bible must be interpreted.* G. K. Chesterton once quipped, "You cannot put a book in the witness-box and ask it what it really means."[6] Interpretation means taking the text and finding the underlying principles of it. We do this in lots of ways, but the good news is that it's not an impossible task. It can be done, faithfully, by *you,* not just Bible scholars and hip pastors. By anyone. God *wants* us to hear Him in His Word.

This means that you have a role to play when you read the Bible, which should flatten you with a great paradox of careful wonder and joy. This is a massive responsibility, and it's going to require you to get out of the interpretive driver's seat and ask a lot of questions of other people. Even though this interpretation is personal, it's not to be done solo. It's not impressionistic, no longer in the territory of "what this means for me."

You're going to need guides. You're going to need to immerse yourself. You're going to need discipline and patience and practice. You're going to have to do some homework. You'll need to do some memorizing and go see some plays and try to get a feel for the big picture—the major action sequences and how the story is moving along as a narrative. You'll need to sit and be frustrated at times while an older couple in front of you is cackling at everything you're missing. You'll need to read more than just one sequence if you want to get to know the language and flow of it. You'll need to read the programs. You'll want to learn some of the trivia. You'll need to learn about the time periods.

The Bible wasn't written to you as the original audience, but it is for you. So to find out what is for you, you'll have to learn about the people who it was written to. You'll have to place yourself in their shoes and learn their stories. You'll have to become selfless and humble.

Third, *there is a right and wrong way to interpret the Bible.* Second Timothy 2:15 reads, "Be diligent to present yourself approved to God . . . rightly dividing the word of truth" (NKJV). The Greek word in that verse for "rightly divide" means "to make a straight cut," like a carpenter making a straight cut on a beam.

The Bible says that there's a right way to handle the Word of truth. What does that imply? That there's a wrong way too. But just because many interpretations of a scripture exist doesn't mean they're *all* automatically flawed or hopelessly beyond understanding.

When you receive a wedding invitation, you don't read for *your* meaning of the invitation; you read for what the bride and groom mean by the invitation. You don't ask yourself *What does*

this invitation mean to me? You ask *Where should I be and at what time?* You understand the cultural rules surrounding invitations and respond accordingly. You don't show up whenever you want, arbitrarily reassigning value to the time of the ceremony based on some sort of intellectually dishonest interpretive theory you've hatched. If you don't understand something—the location, for example, or whether you can bring your significant other—you generally ask someone.

Think about how you have come to the Bible. Maybe you've read it through the "God, fix my life!" lens. Maybe you've read through a "Confirm my theology" lens. What about the "Make my life awesome #blessed" lens or the "Divine power" lens? They each may have their place, but they work by leaving out whatever doesn't confirm their unique perspective. When we come to the Bible, we must continually attempt to drop our agendas and allow it to speak on its own terms. Second Peter 1:20 perfectly summarizes this issue: "No prophecy of Scripture comes from someone's own interpretation." Like understanding *Macbeth,* understanding the Bible is a long-standing group effort of trusted voices, and it *is* possible.

Fourth, *the Bible is the measure of all of God's speech to you.* God will never tell you to do something the Bible says is wrong. The Bible is a lamp to our feet and a light to our path (Psalm 119:105). We use the Scriptures to study our path, not our path to study the Scriptures. Or to borrow from Bruce Waltke, "Ambiguous texts should be interpreted in the light of clear texts."[7]

The Bible clearly says not to steal, so you can confidently conclude that a life of thievery isn't God's will for you. The Bible says not to commit adultery, so you can confidently conclude that

having an affair is not God's perfect plan and will for your . You can also conclude that the voice telling you to do these thing is not from heaven. If you think God hates you and is vindictive, you can read John 3:16 and conclude that God loves you. You can also conclude that the voice that keeps doubting God's love is not from heaven and that it can be shut up with God's Word.

The noise the world, the flesh, and the devil stir up to misdirect us and mess with our feelings must yield to the clear and obvious speech God has already prepared for us in Scripture. There are so many things that a Christian never has to even wonder about because God has already said so much! Our business should be to occupy our minds with what He's already said, because then we can interpret the subjective or unclear with the objective and clear Word of God as it's faithfully interpreted.

From Frustration to Framework

Maybe you've been frustrated in your Bible reading (just like I was frustrated reading *Macbeth*) because sometimes you have no understanding of what the heck is going on. Press through and keep familiarizing yourself with the landscape of the Bible. The more you read Scripture, the more familiar you'll become with it. Every Bible scholar started just like you, in total darkness. But to accelerate your learning, annoy some friends who know more about the Bible than you do! Continually ask them questions about everything you don't know. Also, ask someone you respect and trust which resources they use to read about the Bible, and start learning for yourself.

I believe that God will begin to speak to you through His

Word as you treat it with honor and respect, adding diligence and discipline to your desire to know Him and hear from Him. Don't flip through the pages and then randomly point at a Scripture verse if you're trying to "get a word from God" or make a life decision. I've heard of people doing this and finding some nice Scripture verse, but what about the dude who flipped and pointed to a verse at random, reading Judas "went and hanged himself" (Matthew 27:5)? *Rats,* he thought. So, he tried again, and this time he got, "What you are going to do, do quickly" (John 13:27). Uh, *no.*

That's not how the Bible works; it's not a secret magic book from the library at Hogwarts. It's better and more powerful than that. And as we learn it and sit with it and study it, we become shaped by it over time.

We must learn the Scriptures because God speaks accurately and authoritatively through His Word. The Bible is the measure of all of God's speech. Once we learn the parameters of how He speaks, the types of topics and circumstances He speaks to, and the language He uses, we can hear Him just about anywhere!

The Bible isn't the only way He's going to speak, but it's the primary way. More importantly, it's the *framework* into which He will speak. Scripture is your litmus test for all other sorts of hearing, *and* it creates the grid of meaning and language within you to hear and discern.

A Way to View the World

Let's go back to my niece Frankie for a minute. She's learning our jokes, our humor, and our word choices for a multiplicity of things. Everything we say to Frankie is spoken into a worldview context her father and mother have labored to construct. Someday, when we talk to her about dating, it will no doubt be different from what her friends say about dating. When we talk to Frankie about what it means to love, it will be very different from what Frankie hears at school or on Netflix or from the lyrics of her favorite songs. We'll teach her not only our language but also what these words and concepts and ideas mean. Words carry loads of history that contribute to their particular meaning.

The very best thing a parent can ever give a child is a way in which to view the world. That's what God has given us with the Scriptures. When God says "love" and you say "love," the meanings are typically different. When you're reading the Bible with your narrow lens and reading into the Scriptures what you think love means, you're missing out on the reason God put that word there in the first place. God is speaking, and even though you might be listening, you're not understanding. As you begin to learn the story of redemption, about the person and work of Christ, about what love is in 1 Corinthians 13, and about John the Beloved's letters, you begin to think about God's love in a more holistic way. Sitting in a theater, watching a movie, you see a selfless, biblical *agape* love displayed in a character who gives their life for their friends, and you feel the Holy Spirit stirring deep inside of you and talking to you right there during that movie. You're able to hear God even though it isn't a Christian movie, per se, because your mind has been re-created with godly context.

But even Bible-competent people can miss what God is saying at times. I've found that some of the most stubborn, mean

Christians know the Bible well. Knowing the Bible well doesn't mean you're an angel. As A. W. Tozer mused, "The devil is a better theologian than any of us and is a devil still."[8]

Knowing the Bible and having allowed the Bible to transform you are two very different things. Knowing the Bible and faithfully translating the Bible are also two very different things.

Just as the devil used Scripture to tempt Jesus by taking it out of context, many Christians will take Scripture out of context to either justify their own behavior or beat other people who they don't like over the head with it. Scripture can be misused in innumerable ways.

The Bible is so much bigger than any of us. We're all included, but it's not limited to us. We see what we want to see.

Case in Point

Problem is, people who take Scripture out of context never see their sins in the Bible because they're so blind and self-deceived and because they've cut out of their lives the community that could help them see their issues. It takes *others* to see yourself in Scripture. It takes something different from you. It takes community.

Everybody needs the Bible and others. Everyone needs to learn the Bible *from* others. There's no independence in the kingdom of God. No Wild West. The Bible isn't your six-shooter. You aren't the Lone Ranger.

Everyone is a theologian. *Theo* means "God" and *logia* means "words about," so if you have words about God, you're a theologian. The real question is whether you're a good theologian. A church is always full of theologians. What you want is excellent ones.

Somehow in our world today, the Holy Spirit and the Bible have been pitted against each other. That's like pitting Ronald McDonald against cheeseburgers. The Holy Spirit was involved in the creation of the canon of the Bible. He spoke to the prophets and apostles and helped develop and preserve it. He is God, and He inspired them to take up their pens and write songs, histories, and prophetic stories about His redemption. The Holy Spirit loves the Bible because He made it, and He's always trying to animate and illuminate it, and by that way mature us.

God speaks into your theological framework. Thus, a reading from the church fathers or someone from a traditional background can help bring value to or shed light on Scripture. I highly recommend a reading of G. K. Chesterton's *The Resurrection of Rome,*[9] a book in which Chesterton explains what God has been accomplishing through His church for the last two thousand years.

In some ways we've been guilty of what C. S. Lewis called "chronological snobbery,"[10] a general feeling of disdain for the past because of a sense of progression. We've conflated "new" with "good." You don't need to lean on your own understanding when it comes to Scripture reading. The Holy Spirit will lead you and guide you into all truth, but here's the deal: He often uses others—wise leaders in the faith who have come before us.

I think at some point we need to ask ourselves if our favorite proof text (something out of context) is truly indicative of what God is saying. Okay, I get it—God can speak through anything. He can speak through a donkey, and if He can speak through a donkey, He can speak through a proof text. But that's an exception, and you don't build a life and ministry on an exception; you build on principle.

Are we rightly dividing the Word of Truth? If we aren't, are we representing God correctly?

Forward—Together

We want people to hear God in Scripture, but then we turn them loose like they're teens with *Macbeth* and give them zero instruction, except "What does this mean to you?" That's how people are supposed to hear God?

We all need to compare lenses and broaden the community where we read the Scriptures. Across generations and economic, gender, and racial barriers. Across the boundaries of our traditions, geography, and even history. Because as we compare, the Holy Spirit works through His people to allow a remarkable picture to come into focus. We get to see the story of God play out. We get to hear His voice.

Often people aren't convicted until they're faced with the truth from someone else, whether that's in public preaching and teaching of the Scriptures or in relationship. Rarely do people come to a truthful conclusion on their own. But if we teach people how to read the Bible faithfully and consistently, we can tell them to read the book of John and see fruit and formation in their lives.

In a sense, you should be as overwhelmed by the prospect of being a good theologian as a twenty-year-old should be overwhelmed with the prospect of finding a spouse and a job, caring for pets and having kids, figuring out where to live or what house to buy, and beginning to save for retirement. Developing a God-honoring theological framework is a process you walk through, and it *is* that large with that much scope. Saying anything less cheapens it. Be overwhelmed at times. Don't stop walking through life, and neither should you stop walking through the Bible.

Are you living as though the Bible matters? Are you reading it as though there's real meaning to be discovered?

The Bible is a lot like Shakespeare—it has some of the greatest writing ever and is written to another audience living in a whole different world. But the drama and messages are timeless. God, the greatest author and communicator who ever lived, speaks today through the Bible just as Shakespeare speaks today through *Macbeth.* But it's going to take time to understand it. This doesn't mean we'll never understand it—just that we'll have to be patient as we diligently learn the story and language of the Bible. Eventually, then, after we've been immersed in these stories, this poetry, these songs, this wisdom, we'll hear God clearer than ever.

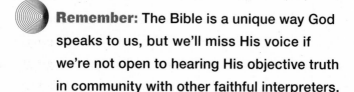 **Remember:** The Bible is a unique way God speaks to us, but we'll miss His voice if we're not open to hearing His objective truth in community with other faithful interpreters.

CHAPTER FIVE

The Myth of the Lone Ranger Christian

It Would Be Easier to Listen If God Didn't Speak Through Messed-Up People So Much

One of the *many* reasons I can't stand social media is that other people are on it. It's *full* of people. To make things worse, they all seem to be just like me. Argumentative. Self-absorbed. Opinionated.

Come to think of it, that's also why I don't like churches—because they're full of people who are, again, just like me. The reason my church isn't perfect is simple: because I'm in it. Nothing gets under my skin as much as annoying people. Once more, people like me.

I suppose we all have our varying degrees of annoyance, although some of us are less aware of how annoying we are. Or putting it a different way, some of us update our social media status with what we're really thinking, and some of us have learned not to but still go on *thinking* the same thing. (Oh, the humanity!)

The very worst, online or in church, is when people start getting up in your business. Like tagging you in flowery Bible verse posts that seem like passive-aggressive hints that you should be nicer. That gets under my skin, which in turn prompts the sarcasm that probably encouraged them to tag me in the first place. Vicious circle.

I'm that kind of Christian as I read my Bible. While I'm reading the book of Proverbs, for example, I'm not thinking about *my* impoverished moral state and how each verse applies to *my* wisdom-lacking life. Just as often I'm thinking about all the people I need to text these verses to. When I read a rebuke in the Bible, I'm not thinking about me. I'm thinking about *you*!

My mother is a bit savage in this regard. I get texts from her *every morning,* while she's doing her devotions. Without fail. She sends me snapshots of passages circled in neon pink highlighter. Usually they're the tragic passages from the Old Testament, about Consequences (yes, with a capital *C*). So-and-so didn't do this and so this *terrible* thing happened to them. (Thanks for the encouraging word, Mum!)

I suppose mums can do that or are even *supposed* to do that. I'm a thirty-five-year-old married man living in another country, but to her I'll always be the genius seventeen-year-old who crashed the family car and still drives too fast. *C'est la vie.*

But even though I poke fun, Mom's early-morning pictures are highlighting a powerful truth. We are all better when we read the Bible in community. *Us* hearing God is exponentially more powerful than *me* hearing Him. It's taken deep relationships to open my heart to what God is saying in the Bible. It's taken people genuinely different from me to point out the truths I could never have seen on my own.

You know, I used to think that hearing God's voice was all about me and my quiet time and my Bible and . . . *me.* But it's always been bigger than me, than any of us. Now I wonder, *What are the principles we need to learn if we're to understand the voice of God through other people? What shifts need to happen in our hearts? How do we discern? How do we build lives open to listening to others? If community is a key way we grow in hearing God, how do we get there?*

Hitched

As with many truths, it took marriage to begin to show me the way. My friend Kevin says, "Marriage is a trick—to make you more like Jesus." I'm beginning to suspect he's right. Do you need marriage to grow? Of course not. Just ask Jesus or Paul or any of the bazillions of single saints throughout history. But a marriage relationship can do a few things for your soul.

That is, if you let it. It's truly not all a honeymoon. You experience all kinds of wonderful joys, but sometimes marriage feels like it's meant to *sanctify* you. Go figure.

If you aren't married, let me describe the experience for you. *My* experience. Do you remember when you were twelve and you'd sleep over at your best friend's house on a three-day weekend or something? The first night was always the *best*—pizza, chips, pop, going to bed super late. Tired? Sure! But you were sugared up and excited out of your mind. You watched movies you didn't generally watch and got candy at a store you didn't usually go to. Everything was new and strange but wonderful.

You woke up the next morning and played all day, and when it was time to go home, you and your friend asked your parents if you could stay another night. They said yes, and you were pumped! Another sleepover! Yay! You got to watch that other movie. But no pizza; you ate regular food. And you ran out of money for pop and chips and candy, so you ate whatever snacks your friend had around. The grown-ups told you not to be so loud, like you were the night before—Dad had an early morning. Sure, everything was great, but the glory had faded a little.

Sometimes you were so bold and delusional as to ask if there could be a *third* sleepover in a row. In the rare case this occurred, it typically turned into a nightmare. You got into a fight with your friend about which movie to watch. You began to miss your mum's cooking. Your friend's parents started to resent your being there. You noticed that their house smelled weird (what *was* that, anyway?). And that third morning when you woke up? You never wanted to get home sooner.

For me, at least, marriage is like the sleepover that never ends. I don't care who you marry, you put two human beings in one house together and there's going to be some friction. Perfect couples don't exist. As far as I'm concerned, marrying the "perfect one" is a myth. Sure, some people will be better matched than others, but no matter who we are, we always marry the wrong person. I mean that in this sense: the moment we start to have disagreements or issues, we begin to think our partner is the problem and that another partner would've been better.

It's better to smash that total illusion with one hard fact: you married a human being.

Marriage is having a person on call twenty-four hours a day to tell you all your issues. This is why half of marriages don't work out. People don't want reality, and they certainly don't want to deal with reality. Marriage is the harshest reality there is. It's an existential ice bath. You never know how messed up you are until you get married. Your parents stop getting all up in your biz sometime in your teens; they don't have the emotional wherewithal to try to undo all the mistakes they made parenting you when you were three, so they sort of give up and hope your friends and your boss and your girlfriend and your spouse and life sort of beat all that stuff out of you.

Your young friends are insecure and typically don't tell you the truth because they're more concerned about being accepted than about being honest. Your girlfriend is also too insecure to upset you; she's tiptoeing around your moody anger problem because she wants to be on your good side and be accepted and keep up appearances about your relationship that ultimately won't matter in the long run. Your job may not matter that much to you in the grand scheme of things, and so you coast, with a boss who deals with problems only when they become crises. You're not a crisis-to-crisis person (yet); you're showing up on time and doing the bare minimum, not attracting any heat.

Then you get married, and everything changes. You can't coast. Say you're a guy. Behaviors she thought were cute before or turned a blind eye to become points of contention and continual conflict. You're messy. But she's late. You're bossy. But she's controlling. You withhold information. But she never stops talking. What's worse is that neither of you knows how to have a conversation without ending up raising your voice and attacking the other's character.

Eventually things come to a head: either you start to work on the relationship by making some changes and getting some help, or things head for the rocks.

If you went for option A where you begin to take responsibility for your shortcomings, follow through on the things that your spouse is holding you accountable for, and open yourself up to an arbitrator or counselor, your life begins to change, slowly but surely. Your reaction time slows down. Every time you're caught doing something wrong, you aren't as defensive. You learn to ask for forgiveness. You learn to forgive. You learn to be a person of your word. You're not personally attacking your spouse every time you have an argument. You both practice lowering your voices. And your life begins to evidence the working of the Holy Spirit.

Because here's the thing: When the sleepover starts to get old, the relationship starts to get real. And that's *incredible*.

The Power of Relationship

First Corinthians 13, the "Love Chapter," was written to the most spiritually gifted church we read about in the New Testament— the crazy Spirit-led church at Corinth, a manic port town overrun with fleshly, self-centered former slaves and Roman soldiers. Many of the former slaves had been born into slavery and had never known self-indulgence like their masters had. Furthermore, the town was full of money, and many of the slaves had so much wealth that they didn't know what to do with themselves. Thus, they lived as though they had twenty lifetimes of partying to do. Their sexual exploits were world renown to the point that "Corinthianize" became a common expression for a pansexual extravaganza.[11]

In many ways the Corinthian church reflected the cultural

climate; the occasion for the writing of the first letter to the Corinthians was to correct a man who was having sex with his stepmother. Secondarily, Paul had to address and bring order to the Corinthians' contemptible corporate gatherings.

Paul's letter highlights the incredible happenings among them, but there was also horrible sin. The basics of holiness and justice were not in place. Their total lack of spiritual maturity was destroying the church. Spiritually gifted does not mean spiritually mature.

Coming back to our first chapter in this book, God is a good Father, and part of His desire to speak to us is directly connected to our overall growth and maturity. His communication grows clearer as we are matured, and so He will speak to our maturity for long and extended seasons. You can read 1 Corinthians 13 all you want, but until you allow someone to explain that what you're doing is not loving, you will never see yourself as the person needing to "hear" 1 Corinthians 13.

The clanging cymbal theme of 1 Corinthians 13 is an illustration of the cacophony the Corinthians' worship services had created. Paul knew the cure for them was *agape* love—unconditional, no strings attached. But *agape* love isn't a love you hear about and then easily perform. It's worked out over time in community. It requires "facing the music" and responding to confrontation. Was the Spirit at work and speaking to the Corinthians? Yes—in the form of a letter from their pastor abroad, Paul the apostle.

The fruit of the Spirit—the way you can tell the Holy Spirit is evident in someone's life—is love, joy, peace, patience, kindness, goodness, faithfulness, gentleness, and self-control. All this is continually tested and developed in the furnace of *relationships*. You know, the kind of relationships that happen when you get past the candy and movies and figure out what it means to live together forever.

The Corinthians were nervous about seeing Paul because he was the only one who would tell it straight to them. He was their father in the Lord. Paul reminds them of this in his first letter to them, saying, "You have a zillion teachers, but you have few fathers" (1 Corinthians 4:15, paraphrase mine).

Proverbs 27:6 says, "Wounds from a friend can be trusted, but an enemy multiplies kisses" (NIV). You see, the degree to which other people love us is the degree to which they will be truthful with us. Their friendship determines their willingness to give us a "wound" with the truth. I'm thankful for my wife, Jasmine, who loves me enough to tell me the truth I need to hear but never *want* to hear. God loves me, and because He loves me, He plants me in relationships. He gave Jasmine and me to each other to hear His voice together.

The righteous are referred to throughout the Bible as trees that are the "planting of the LORD" (Isaiah 61:3). Whether you're married, single, or dating, God wants to plant you in relationships you can't get out of. He wants you to be in rich and reciprocal community with believers who can help mature you and whom you can help mature. He wants you to hear Him through others, and He wants to speak to others through you. That's what the church is all about.

Jesus said, "Unless a grain of wheat falls into the earth and dies, it remains alone" (John 12:24). He was talking about Himself in that passage, but the principle, in nature and in the spiritual life, is true. Sometimes relationships feel as though you're buried alive and slowly dying—because that's what's happening! You're being suffocated. You have no space. Your patience is being tested. And you'll have opportunity after opportunity to learn to respond correctly! Eventually that annoying, selfish part of you will be dead and buried with Christ, and a new you will be raised in power.

My wife is one of the clearest voices from God that I can hear. Her wounds are faithful; they are loving and consistent. She wants the best for me, and she's close enough to me to see what's holding me back. She's a voice I can trust. God has put her in my life to grow me up. God has planted me into my marriage. At times it feels as though I'm dying—because I am!

Your closest community needs to play a role in your spiritual life; played rightly, it's an invaluable role. They hold up a mirror to your face and help you see what you truly look like. You become increasingly aware of your true condition. You now see yourself as the fool in the book of Proverbs. You see *yourself*, not just *that guy*.

God speaking through my community encourages me to hear Him elsewhere. Revelation builds on revelation. The Scriptures begin to come alive and wound me, just as my wife wounds me. And the Scriptures are faithful to wound and bind up.

Maturing Relationships

An inherent wisdom exists in external voices, and when those external voices are godly and love you, they ought to be considered.

These sources become the foundation of God's wisdom toward us as we recognize and listen to them. Proverbs 18:1 says, "A man who isolates himself seeks his own desire; he rages against all wise judgment" (NKJV). You don't need to be the Lone Ranger Christian when you have the right people around you. It's hearing God for dummies, it's safe, it's more objective, and it's biblical.

As my dad powerfully states, "Spiritual maturity does not happen outside the context of relationships." It just doesn't. It takes people to tell you that you have problems, and then you begin to see your problems in Scripture. That's the process of growing up spiritually—putting away childish things.

We must rethink how and why God speaks to us. Because if it's true that we grow spiritually through our relationships, then several things follow. First, this places a greater value on God-ordained relationships (for you theology nerds, maybe even a "sacramental" value). Second, it balances out an overfocus on God's voice being only an internal dialogue. And third, it demands we become humble listeners in all of life if we want to hear God.

We need to accept that we aren't always going to agree with everyone. We need to learn that sometimes we should just have a high confidence that God's brought someone we disagree with into our life rather than putting such a high value on agreement. Agreement is overrated. Maybe you don't know everything. The entire point of having someone like this in your life is that it drives you to the admission that you *don't know everything*.

"Who has God brought into my life?" That's the question we should keep coming back to, to properly prioritize and give weight to God's speech toward us through other people.

Do I really believe God put me in this marriage, that it's not just my doing? Do I believe God has given me this person who loves me despite all my issues? If I do, then maybe I need to begin to listen to what this person is saying to me.

Do I truly believe God has given me this amazing business partner? Yes, I do! I remember the tears and prayers, begging God to bring somebody just like this into my life. *God,* I prayed, *send help! Send someone who can help me with this business!* And along came this person.

Let's go back to the beginning: Do we really believe this person is a God-send? If the answer is yes, then the God-send is going to have a God-word.

Do I truly believe God put this doctor in my life? Do I really believe that? Is this doctor an answer to when I shouted, "Lord, heal me!"? If the answer is yes, then I need to get with the program and begin to follow through on doctor's orders, treating them as though they *are* God's words to me.

Instead of seeing people in the natural—getting too familiar with the gift they are from the Lord—we need to begin to see them as people God has placed in our lives to speak the truth and bring the blessing of God as we show enough humility to receive it and engage it.

I'm not saying we should take everything they say as *inerrant;* I'm saying we should have enough humility to recognize that these are the types of people we asked God for, and when they open their mouths, we should listen to what they're saying, hear it, and contemplate it.

People who have few strong personal relationships are often

living in a fantasy, completely and totally out of touch with themselves and the way they're perceived. Many times they're out of touch with reality. God will give us people who will ground us in the truth about ourselves and our situation—that which accords with reality. Within this context we can "hear" God's specific will. It isn't just that He can't communicate to people who are out of touch with reality, but that they can't comprehend what He's saying. When we reject the voices in our lives put there to bring godly humility, God begins to resist us. James 4:6 says, "God resists the proud, but gives grace to the humble" (NKJV).

Hearing God becomes less about what we want and more about what He wants in these types of relationships. The very nature of true relationships is that we cannot manipulate others. Spouses can be manipulated at times, but they're smart and won't take it for long. Most parents or pastors who love you and have their heads screwed on straight won't be manipulated either. They will insist on being heard, and they'll stick to their guns. This places us, the hearers, in a difficult and vulnerable spot, because we can't be the great manipulators of God's voice when it's coming through others. We're the ones always saying, "God told me to do this," and it's almost always something convenient. But when what God says comes through others, we can't provide a "God told me, and guess what! It's exactly what I wanted all along."

Oh, God told you to stay home from work and watch Netflix? Must be nice. I rarely hear people say, "God told me to ask my boss to forgive me because of the rotten attitude I've had toward him." That's rare, because maturity is rare.

So these become the questions: Are we in the kind of relationships where God can say the hard, good things? Do we have friends around us who are kind enough to wound us in love? Pray for relationships that will be the voice of God in your life and faithfully wound you and speak the truth to you. If you're wondering if you have the kind of friend you can go deep with and grow in Christ alongside, try to recollect if one of your friends has ever challenged you. If so, that friend's the one. Ask them to speak into your life if they see something that requires growth or repentance. The closest relationships—with mentors, spouses, committed friends—shape us most.

Ephesians 4:11–15 tells us that Christ gave some to be apostles, prophets, evangelists, pastors, and teachers for the building up of the saints, speaking the truth in love so that we may grow up into Christ, who is the head. The Bible doesn't get any clearer on hearing God through other people than that.

Real Relationships

Many types of relationships can bring the kind of unique maturity that makes another person God's voice to us. They can be peers or people we mentor or care for (kids are incredible, honest teachers), and they can be the kinds of people we think of as spiritual fathers or mothers.

Not everything these people say to us is necessarily from God. Sometimes what they tell us is just their wisdom. Occasionally it may be totally off base. But sometimes the Spirit uses a word from another person to highlight an area of growth in our lives in ways that are so incredible it must be from God. When you hear it, you just know. You just do.

Let's focus on the voices of mentors and leaders for the rest of this chapter, since every Christian is called to have those roles. We don't do this thing alone; we're called to have spiritual parents.

Spiritual mothers and fathers don't speak only to character issues; they speak to maturity. And because of that, they also speak to identity, calling, and direction. Spiritual parents bring clarity to these major questions and help us along our way. This clarity doesn't come from their being infallible or perfect people. It comes from the fact that Jesus has given them a gift for this. It comes from the fact that they know the Scriptures and can deliver God's Word over our lives directly, with authority and precision. And it comes because they're not novices but rather experienced people who have been around the block.

Because they've walked through short-term storms that bring all kinds of doubts and insecurities, spiritual mothers and fathers can see past them. They speak God's mobilizing grace, helping us through the analysis paralysis and to burst through halting anxiety.

When we have trouble remembering who we are and what we're supposed to be doing, they remind us of the words God has spoken over our lives. They help us stir our faith in God's direction, confirming that we're headed in the right direction.

Spiritual mothers and fathers aren't trying to champion their own cause or agenda; they're championing the work God is doing in our hearts. Like all good parents, they don't seek anything for themselves; they aren't in it for personal gain, because the win for us is a win for them! But just as with any maturing or close relationship, this is exactly why they're so hard to listen to sometimes. Our pride and immaturity tempt us to reject and run from their wisdom. Their wisdom is different. It's usually hard. It's what we need, and that nearly always yanks us from what we want in the moment.

In the same way I needed a guide as a toddler—someone to tell me "Don't play in the road" or "Don't smoke cigars in your crib until midnight" (kidding, who smokes cigars as a three-year-old? I'm not Dutch)—I need guides as an adult. In the same way my parents' protective and informative voice in my life was God's, so can a spiritual father's or mother's voice be God's voice for me. And for you too.

Flawed but Faithful

Maybe some of you have had terrible parents, and the idea of giving someone a parental role in your life again is terrifying. You know firsthand that people are flawed, and especially if you have an abusive background, the idea of letting someone in is equated to allowing someone to use or misuse you.

If this is you, my heart breaks and reaches out to you. The journey of faith to trust that another person can be the voice of God to you is harder than for someone who has never been wounded in those close relationships.

Consider the Corinthian story again. The real miracle of the Corinthian narrative is that Paul identified as their spiritual father and fought to be their father against fake leaders who were trying to undermine his leadership. If I were Paul and someone walked up to me and said, "Hey, man—you know that church you planted and pastor over in Corinth? It's a total mess. Everyone gets hammered at church, they've all divided into warring factions like a soccer fan club in Brazil, and one dude is sleeping with his stepmom, and no one's saying anything about it. Oh, and they shout over one another for attention when they're preaching," I'd be like, "Um, Corinth? Never been there. Interesting. Yeah, I've never even heard of them. Not my church. Probably John Mark's plant. Got to watch out for JM; he's a pretty lazy leader." But Paul doesn't do that. Instead, he steps in as a patient spiritual parent.

You see, good parents are insanely patient with their kids, because they know their own flaws. Because they're faithful. Patience is first on the "Love List" that Paul writes to the Corinthians, and he was a great example of it toward them. He was able to show patience because he had experienced it (1 Timothy 1:16). God the Father was patient with Paul when Paul was Saul, and Saul was killing Christians. Paul, having received incredible grace, was able to give incredible grace. Flawed and faithful go together. Always.

But just as a spiritual parent has qualities, we sons and daughters have responsibilities. We shoulder responsibility for our growth. Here are some of the basics to help hear God through maturing relationships.

First, *we need to be willing to listen, and then consider and implement change.* We can't be know-it-alls. Pride is the opposite of maturity. We have an obligation to listen openly and earnestly. We can't be impatient because we don't understand directions. How are you going to hear God's voice through other people if you dismiss them or if you won't sit still and admit that you don't know everything? We must show humility.

Second, *we need to be vulnerable.* We need to be willing to talk about our root issues and not just peripherals. If you can't be vulnerable with a doctor and say where it *really* hurts, you'll never get a proper diagnosis. How are you going to get godly wisdom if you're unwilling to let someone else into the truth? Once again, this is a huge act of humility, and that's perfect, because God is attracted to humility. Remember, He resists the proud but gives grace to the humble. He speaks to the lowly.

And third, *we need to be honoring.* We typically dishonor people because we think we're smarter or better than they are. When we don't value them, it leads to all kinds of dishonoring behaviors. But if we dishonor others, we'll almost never hear God's voice because we've put ourselves at the center of our universe.

Jesus said if we honor a prophet in the name of a prophet, we'll receive a prophet's reward (Matthew 10:41). Be respectful. If someone is giving to you of their wisdom, value their time. Be thankful. Be grateful. Treat them like a servant of Jesus.

Are you noncommunicative? Stubborn? Proud? Passive? Aggressive? Untruthful? Are you honoring people the way they ought to be honored? Are you approachable? Can these wise voices tell you exactly what they think? Or do they need to walk on eggshells around you? Are you interested in change and transformation? Or are you just putting on a show? Are you aware that spiritual fathers and mothers go for heart issues? That's why they exist. Are you frustrating them by playing it safe and shallow?

Do you follow through with the assignments you're given? Are you learning the building blocks you've been asked to learn, completing the exercises? Maybe change isn't happening because you aren't doing the work. Can you honestly say you've implemented their instructions with all your energy? As people say, "You gotta do the work."

I'm still learning, all the time. But when I'm around someone I admire or respect, someone who's been around for a while, I absolutely expect God to speak to me through them. My honor helps draw His voice out of them. I honor what God has put in them and how they have honored the call of God in their lives. I don't take them for granted. I see the great value of their life and calling. I ask them questions, because I refuse to be proud, and I believe God will speak to me through them. I'm choosing not to allow our anti-authority culture to creep into my attitude and hijack God's plan for my life. I'm choosing to reject that in exchange for something better.

Practice Makes Passion

What godly relationships do you have? Are your parents full of wisdom? God can use parents who aren't even Christians to speak wisdom to us. How about a spouse or a close friend? Roommate? Professor? Coworker? Is your life open to hearing what you don't necessarily like to hear from them? Or are you the type of person to cut someone off (or even out of your life) when they challenge you? You aren't just cutting *them* off; you're probably cutting off God's voice.

This is a difficult journey, and one of the hardest things about hearing God through maturing relationships is that it doesn't—*can't*—happen overnight. Learning to hear God well takes time, and taking time is hard to handle if you're impatient like me.

These voices in your life are uncomfortable gold. The price you pay for not having them is repeating mistakes over and over until you become so overwhelmed by life that you give up your dreams, or that people necessary for those dreams to come to fruition give up on you. As you yield to the wisdom and structure these voices bring, God begins to pour so much value and strategy into your life that it's like the best of both worlds: your youth and someone else's experience.

Therefore, we need persistence—that grit that keeps us from quitting. Quitting is what spiritual infants do, and it's what good fathers and mothers do *not* allow when something important is at stake. Good parents teach their children that discipline in the right direction leads to delight, and that life yields to those who refuse to give up.

When I was nine, I told my dad I wanted to play piano. He told me he would buy the family a piano, but for one year I'd have to commit to taking piano lessons that he'd pay for. As a dumb nine-year-old, I didn't understand the implications of such a binding oral contract, and so I foolishly and immediately said, "Yes!"

Three months later, reality set in. I was up to my eyeballs in stupid scales and nursery rhyme piano charts, and I was utterly underwhelmed by my musical prowess. I'd pictured myself a Mozart. I was playing like, well, *like a kid.* Summer had come, and my friends were all playing outside in the evenings. But when Dad came home from work, he would ask if I had practiced for thirty minutes that day. If the answer was no, he would march me to the piano. I remember crying over it one hot summer evening, with my father behind me—arms folded—as I rehearsed "Auld Lang Syne" in genuine bitterness and agony of soul.

Not too many weeks after mastering "Auld Lang Syne," I found a piece of music titled "Eleanor Rigby," and I fell in love with piano for myself. That hot July night I hadn't been ready for "Eleanor Rigby." I had to come through "Auld Lang Syne" to get to "Eleanor Rigby." I needed my father to be the "helper of my joy" and hold my feet to the fire. I needed him to remind me who I was: his beloved son. And what it meant to be his son—a man of discipline, a man of obligation and responsibility. I needed him to tell me what my direction was—to the living room to practice my craft again. I needed all this so I could arrive at the sheer bliss of being able to play a song sung by the Beatles. I fell out of love with the piano, but my father taught me the discipline of perseverance, and then I fell in love with the piano again, so passionately that I have never looked back.

This is what God's voice, by the Holy Spirit and through spiritual relationships, will do to your love for Jesus—it will set you ablaze with a spiritual passion so fervent that you'll know the clarity of calling. You will grow. You will get stronger. You will experience beauty you never knew existed.

And you might begin to create beauty yourself.

Remember: God speaks to us through the maturing voices of those around us. Without humility and persistence, we will not hear Him.

CHAPTER SIX

The Myth of "Don't Worry! Nothing Weird Will Happen!"

Why Don't We Want to Talk About Prophecy?

Do not despise prophecies.

—1 Thessalonians 5:20

I want you all to speak in tongues,
but even more to prophesy.

—1 Corinthians 14:5

Just mention the word *prophecy* and you'll get a whole smorgasbord of reactions from Christians. You'll get theological definitions from the Bible nerds, applause from the charismatics, raised eyebrows from the Reformed crowd, lottery numbers from the prosperity preachers, and stares from everyone else.

I was raised in a wild charismatic church run by zealous, beautiful Jesus freaks. "Prophecy" to us?

Beautiful.

Moving.

Constant.

Let's start with a little background. My parents were both drugged-out hippies who got saved in the early seventies' Jesus People movement at a Teen Challenge coffeehouse (a hangout where Jesus freaks, Jesus-loving hippies, sang folk songs about Jesus).

Then they started going to a crazy Latter Rain independent charismatic church (speaking in tongues, dancing, conga lines, one-hour preservice prayer meetings followed by an hour of worship that consisted of three songs sung for twenty minutes each, followed by an hour or two of preaching, followed by a long sweaty altar call, followed by a potluck, followed by an evening service that repeated the exact same thing into all hours of the night). My parents never went home between services on Sundays. They picnicked at the church all day. The Christian school attached to the church didn't have school on Mondays. Why? Because everyone had a church hangover on Mondays, having been at the church all day on Sundays. *Literally. All day.*

They were attracted to the church because of the vibrant worship—electric guitars and drums—and the incessant twenty-four-hours-a-day community all those weirdo hippies craved (and needed). Every service had open-mic-style "prophecy"—and it would go on for what sometimes felt like an eternity.

I have this theory that the Charismatic Renewal—all the way from the seventies to the nineties—happened because some of the baby boomer generation (the ones who keep Tommy Bahama restaurants in business; buy condos in Jupiter, Florida, and Scottsdale, Arizona; and talk about how the Eagles played "real music") are a bunch of hippies who just want to do hippy things. They love California jam bands with twelve-minute interludes, so they re-created that in their church music and experience. My theory is that charismatics aren't weird; *hippies* are weird. And it just so happens that most charismatics in recent memory were ex-hippies.

I'll be the first to admit that I'm a hippie too. Sure, I've been a bit reactionary to the way my loving parents did church (and life), maybe because I grew up under the chairs in churches and restaurant tables, where they would pray and prophesy and yack and yack for hours on end. My parents have always been "If the doors of the church are open, we are there an hour early and an hour after" type of people. But it didn't end there; they always brought all that praying and prophesying home with them.

It was painful, mainly because of their enthusiasm. Every Monday they started family devotions by singing some worship songs (with the windows and doors wide open, so the entire neighborhood could hear us—it was so embarrassing), and then they moved into a jam session of "free praise," when my dad made us all speak in tongues and sing spontaneous songs while lifting our hands. He'd say to me, sternly, "Louder, son. Louder. *Louder.* Lift your hands. Louder!" If one of us three kids didn't feel like singing loudly or we started crying (this happened at least every other Monday), he shut down the meeting and went into a teaching moment about the trichotomy of the soul and how David wrote throughout the Psalms, "I *will* praise the Lord" (emphasis mine). Then he expounded on how to "set" one's will to worship God before making us stand up and try the thing on. "Louder, son—*louder.*"

Then there was the prophetic word training and activations. My dad eventually became a traveling teacher/prophet and ran courses on prophetic ministry. Our Monday family devotions were his laboratory, and we were his guinea pigs. I sat in silence as Dad made each of us share something we thought God was saying. This was my childhood.

When the Toronto Blessing hit in 1994 (and I wish I was referencing the Blue Jays winning the World Series that year, but I'm not), we were at the ground zero of that charismatic revival, since we lived just outside of Toronto. As though the charismatic world weren't strange enough, it was as if the ghost of Walt Disney came over our strange already-Jesus-freak church and sprinkled people repellant on us.

Basically, everything got *longer.*

When our church leadership eventually began to "break up" with the nineties and fell in love with discipleship models from South America, I took off for Bible college and four years of "Who am I?" contemplation.

All that to say, if you think "Holy Spirit" people and spiritual gifts like prophesying can be weird (or can even hurt people, or whatever else you can imagine), take it from me—it *can* be weird! I've seen it all.

Prophecy done wrong can be harmful and abusive. (Just like anything spiritual, by the way: preaching, teaching, or worshiping.) And prophecy done *right* can rule! It comes back to the human element. Typically, when people have an issue with churches or spiritual gifts, they just have an issue with what people have done wrong. It's like hating burritos because you got sick from leftover Taco Bell one time. Don't judge it all based on one bad experience.

The Baby and the Bathwater

Still, I suppose we all have had our experiences—like I did—with "prophecy." They can result in anything from dismissing it entirely to metaphorically guzzling it like holy Mountain Dew. Our experiences often define and limit our attitudes and perspectives—how we think of prophecy when it comes to mind. I used to think *long, boring, awkward, and for hippies* when I thought of prophecy in church. But I can't allow that to dictate my thoughts and feelings now, because prophecy is just too biblical and valuable to the church. Both the myth that prophecy is dead and the myth that it's a goofy free-for-all are false. There's a middle way, and God speaks to us through it.

I must allow the main thrust of Scripture, particularly Paul's letters to the Corinthians (and from there, and only in this order, look at the Acts narratives), to define what prophecy is. In the Old Testament, prophecy is a role for the Jewish nation and an activity people sometimes did to pass on a message from God. They took it seriously—as in, if someone spoke for God and what they said didn't happen, they'd be killed.

Killed.

Dead.

Not metaphorically, like by an outraged Twitter mob. Literally. Smooshed by *crowds of people with large rocks.*

Prophecy in the New Testament is different. It's Spirit-inspired utterance for encouragement, guidance, and comfort. It may include a predictive or confirmational element given by the Holy Spirit to help guide and direct God's people. The apostle Paul directs Christians to earnestly desire this spiritual gift because of its encouraging nature to the church. We are supposed to want it.

Many people think prophecy requires no biblical foundation. In some people's minds, the Holy Spirit and His giftings are somehow unrelated to the Bible, which He inspired, and its teachings. In their minds, you don't need to know the Bible to prophesy and to do so well. This being the case, prophecy has by and large received a bad rap because it's been generally demonstrated by lazy Christians with bad theologies. Many local church prophecies are strange because people's theologies are strange. Many local church prophecies are harsh because people's theologies are harsh.

Another myth about prophecy is that it must be delivered in a particular style. It needs to be spoken authoritatively, with old King James English, and shouted maniacally, like a frenzied street preacher. Prophecy doesn't belong to your tambourine-smacking grandmother or your hippie flower-child friend. It belongs to you. Normal, everyday people can be stirred by the Holy Spirit to speak an encouraging word that's biblically sound in a loving, gentle, and normal way to anyone. As we learn to respond to the Holy Spirit's leading, we can grow in our ability to hear supernaturally both what the Spirit wants to speak and how He wants to speak it.

So much is at stake here. You see, at its root, prophecy today is like the inner voice of the Spirit but for the sake of *others*. Most of us know that feeling, that nudge of inner insight when God's Spirit speaks directly to our hearts. It's like that—quiet, different, needing to be trusted. But it's for someone else.

My friend Paul once told me about a conversation he had with a pastor. The pastor asked if the Spirit was saying anything to Paul about his situation. After thinking about it for a minute, my pal replied, "Yeah, but it's weird."

"Lay it on me," the pastor replied.

"Well, the Spirit's saying you're like a Labrador retriever. Faithful. Present. Just happy to *be* with God. And that makes God happy too."

The guy he was talking to got quiet (usually a sign that the

Spirit *has* said something). "You don't know how much that means to me," he said. "I just lost my Lab. He was the best friend you could imagine. That picture is exactly what I needed to hear about God's love for me."

What? Comparing this guy to a dog was God's way of speaking a prophecy of life over him? You bet it was.

Who said this Christian thing wasn't going to get, you know, *weird*?

God can say so much in this unique and totally weird way. So many little personal things, with that raise-the-hair-on-your-arms kind of timing. So many little moments that make you go, *Huh—I guess this is real, after all.*

Exploring a Broader Biblical Definition

Prophecy is (or ought to be) doctrinally correct, lovingly spoken, uniquely appropriate, and encouragingly focused words that originate from the Holy Spirit, are spoken into the life of a believer by another believer, and produce life-giving, Jesus-loving, biblical faith and hope.

If that's the definition of prophecy, every single Christian simply *must* experience it—at least in my opinion. Why wouldn't you want to? Why wouldn't you want that incredible, personal faith-building experience of feeling seen by God's own Spirit, not only as part of the church but also for who you are?

My conviction is that we must create avenues for everyone to experience that. Paul's great desire for the Corinthians is that, more than anything else, they learn to prophesy. He urges this after his Love Chapter. Why? Because love isn't silent; it's audible. Everything about God and especially the fact that we have a Bible is proof of that. God speaks because He loves. A loving church is a prophetic church—a church that calls out the God-destiny and edifies itself.

If you share my opinion, you'll like this good news: Prophecy isn't getting less popular; it's getting more popular. It's become quite trendy, mainly because charismatic churches and their conferences are the fastest growing worldwide. Prophecy doesn't belong only to charismatics; it belongs to all Christians, especially to Christians who know the Bible and are moved by the Holy Spirit to love other Christians. That should include everyone who knows Jesus.

Our culture, for the most part, is in an encouragement deficit. We're the most discouraged and depressed we've ever been. Suicide rates are on the rise. Sermons and cheery Instagram photos with Bible verses aren't enough. People need personalized encouragement, and God knows this, which is why He's given this gift to the church and wants everyone to desire to walk in it! Somebody's breakthrough is on the other side of your prophetic encouragement.

Now think about the Acts narrative. In Acts 1, the disciples are asking Jesus if ethnic Israel and David's kingdom are going to be restored. Their whole world is self-focused. Jesus heads out, and they go to the upper room to wait. They're nervous and unsure about what to do next. Then tongues of fire come on their heads. The next minute, they're out in the streets, preaching the gospel in different languages. Think about this from a forty-thousand-foot level. One minute they're waiting to drive the Gentiles out of the Holy Land; the next minute they're preaching to the Gentiles in their respective native tongues, filled with the Holy Spirit.

Let's not get lost in the detail of the supernatural aspect of instantly learning a new language. Let's think about this thematically: The Holy Spirit teaches us how to speak other languages. Sometimes this is literal. Sometimes metaphorical. But the Spirit helps translate the message of love to be received.

It's that simple. The Holy Spirit, according to Thomas Aquinas, is the love of God.[12] Jesus is the Logos (the Word), and the Spirit is the love. The love of God shed abroad in our hearts by the Holy Spirit bursts outward, putting a God-sized desire in us to connect with others and pour God's love into their hearts. That's how prophecy works. It's a Holy Spirit urge within us to spread the love of God in our hearts to others. That's why everyone should desire to prophesy, as Paul begged. It unites us to God's people through God's Spirit of love.

Have you ever received a prophetic word of encouragement? You probably have. Maybe you didn't even know it. God loves to encourage us through others who have a gift of speaking godly hope and faith. While I'm never looking around for a prophetic word (or hoping to get one), they tend to come to me because I tend to hang out with prophetic people in prophetic atmospheres. Prophetic people are full of God's Word and vision. They're excited about what God is doing now, and they can't stop talking about it because they're a part of it, and they want you to be a part of it too. Therefore, they're always calling it out in others. My friends and I are prophetic that way because we keep ourselves excited about what God is doing. Our church is the same way. We love what God is doing and saying now. We need fresh, and we speak fresh.

The Prophet

Most prophetic people in the Old Testament weren't like Moses—they didn't have face-to-face revelation from God Himself (Numbers 12:6–8). First Peter 1:10 tells us that "the prophets who prophesied about the grace that was to be yours searched and inquired carefully." The overarching idea is that the prophets then were like us today. Unlike Moses and the disciples and Paul, we haven't had the privilege of FaceTime with God. We've needed to rely on what has already been revealed to Moses, the disciples, and Paul as our framework for understanding God's continuing speech.

What Peter necessarily implies is that the prophets of the Old Testament were the theological heavies of their day. It was their job to remind the people of God of their covenantal commitments (Torah). They had to know the law of Moses cold. They had to speak it accurately at a moment's notice into a specific set of circumstances.

Much of prophecy today has been relegated to a single expression that is almost always spontaneous and ecstatic. But Peter gives us a different vantage point of Old Testament prophetic ministry, that the prophets "searched and inquired." These men, who were writers, wrote down many of their prophetic words. Additionally, they were theologians who had completely absorbed

Torah, writing in the context of the existing Mosaic framework as inspired by the Holy Spirit for each unique circumstance. They were the guardians of God's Word, and their job was to remind Israel of its covenant with God as well as uniquely apply God's present words within the existing covenant.

In the same way, I believe prophetic people are first and foremost called to be conscious caretakers and audible signposts of salvation history, like the prophets of the Old Testament were. A prophetic sense of "now" comes from what God did "then." If you think you have a prophetic gift, you should become the best theologian you can be. You should know the Bible inside and out. You should be totally familiar with the major themes and motifs of Scripture. The clear revealed will and Word of God is the context the Holy Spirit wants to speak into and for you to speak from. Good theology equals good prophetic word. Bad theology equals bad prophetic word.

Whether or not we're aware of it, prophecy is always received and given through a theological lens—the lens of salvation history. This is exactly what gives prophecy its meaning and potency. But it isn't the only lens around. Far from it. And just like the image we see in the Corinthian church, we can fall prey to the danger of competing lenses—when we're coloring the real message God is giving to the point that sharing it is worse than not sharing it at all.

The Holy Spirit isn't going to fix your bad theology with a prophetic word. No, you'll need to do what everyone else has done and get your read on, humble yourself, study, and learn from others. As Paul reminds us, "The spirits of prophets are subject to prophets" (1 Corinthians 14:32). The Holy Spirit doesn't put you into a trance and hijack your brain and mouth when you prophesy over people. You are in control of the words coming out of your mouth. You are responsible for those words as well. And because you're in control and responsible for those words, that hints at the idea that you can prophesy effectively (and grow in that effectiveness)—or not.

Back to Sons and Daughters

Aren't even *kids* supposed to be prophesying in the last days? Joel foretold that God will pour out His Spirit on all flesh and that our sons and daughters will prophesy (2:28)! So isn't that the dream? Everyone walking around with the fire hose, melting off one another's faces with prophetic awesomeness? And can the Holy Spirit speak through kids who have a prophetic word? Well yes, but that's not the norm. Why? Because God is a good Father, and He loves the processes that bring maturity. That's the whole *point* of this. Remember?

Before we go on, let's bring some further clarity to prophecy in general. It can roughly be divided into two categories—foretelling and forth-telling.

Foretelling is probably more unique and exceptional; it happens, but not everyone has this type of gift, and it takes a great deal of development. Also, God tends to have this thing about not telling us exactly what's going to happen, which requires faith. Sometimes He gives us little bits and pieces of the massive puzzle, to create faith and expectation or to point us in the right direction.

But once again, directional *You're going to marry this person* type stuff is just not God's preferred modus operandi. To even operate prophetically with that type of instinct or understanding is to miss such a large biblical narrative that you might as well just stop turning people upside down.

Revelation 19:10 gives us an important little hint about prophecy, saying, "The testimony of Jesus is the spirit of prophecy." This golden nugget, corresponding with the rest of Scripture, indicates that most prophecy is about forth-telling. In short, it reminds people who Jesus is in the face of adversity and discouragement. It points to the example of Jesus when we're trying to figure out what to do, how to do it, and why to do it.

Forth-telling reminds us what Jesus has already done for us and of the hope we can have for tomorrow. It reminds us that Jesus is God and we are not. Prophecy is all about pointing to Jesus and encouraging people in Jesus.

In the same way, to build hope, the Old Testament prophets would memorize the Scriptures (the narrative of God's faithfulness in the past), consider and work through the major themes theologically, be in right relationship with the community of God, and—as led by the Spirit of God in an attitude of humility, love, and encouragement formed by a practical theology of the church and the bond of the Spirit—declare and sometimes personalize prophecies over people's lives!

While we should earnestly desire to prophesy and not despise prophecy, we need to realize that not every prophetic word is completely accurate and that all of prophecy needs to be judged. As with anything we're considering a "word from God," we need to submit to the Bible, the wisdom and counsel of others, our pastors and leaders, time and processes, and ultimately God Himself. Psalm 105:19 says, "Until what he had said came to pass, the word of the LORD tested him." God's prophetic promises aren't always a guarantee of success: they're a reminder to stay faithful to His path, knowing that as we are obedient and patient, He will bring His word to pass. The prophetic most often comes to encourage our diligence in the things of God. Prophecy, then, like all of Christianity, marries inner spiritual instinct to godly rational intellect.

Speaking to Destiny

The prophetic is always about speaking to destiny, and our destiny has always been and will always be to grow into the image of Jesus Christ. Words that point people into the formation of Christ by means of the Holy Spirit are the entire point of prophecy. And for some reason, the words I speak over myself have more impact when they come from someone else—a pastor, a friend, the community of God. That's prophecy—*someone else* reminding me that my entire future, the discovery of who I really am, is becoming more like Jesus. This is what God's voice in maturing relationships sounds like when it comes from the broader body, not from only one trusted spiritual friend.

The prophetic insight, the *message* for every single situation, doesn't change, no matter what the specifics are. The message is my Christlikeness. No matter what's said, it's in service of that growing maturity. The main thrust of God's voice must be the main thrust of prophecy—that God is primarily speaking to *how* rather than to *what*. The *what* is love. Just read 1 Corinthians 13 again.

Prophecy needs to get back to Jesus in a big way and let its focus be on the ultimate destination the Spirit Himself bears witness to: that we, despite all our flaws and failings, are predestined to be conformed to the image of Jesus. We hear Him better as we become more like Him.

It takes grace to give, and it takes grace to receive. A well-known friend of mine just could *not* take a compliment. He had no idea what to do when someone came up to him and thanked him for a song he'd written or a performance he'd given. He didn't know how to process it. I remember how awkward he got because he didn't want people to fall into hero worship. But he was making the exchange difficult and awkward for sincere people who were authentically thankful for him and were simply trying to express their heartfelt gratitude. A mentor of mine once told me that we need to learn the grace of receiving and that a compliment is like a rose, extended toward us. All we need to do is receive kindly. It takes a learned grace to receive well.

I have another friend who's extremely well known. We were recently at a restaurant together, and I couldn't believe how thoughtful and kind he was toward those who expressed their admiration and thanks. It's absolutely exhausting to be that dialed in and receptive toward people, but he carried it so authentically and generously that I thought, *Wow! That is gracious!*

Finding and putting yourself in prophetic atmospheres are simple. Find people who love Jesus, love others, love what God is doing in their community, and are vocal about it. Then put yourself in their community. That's it. In no time you'll start to be a recipient and giver of Holy Spirit encouragement. This is how the Holy Spirit builds churches on a molecular level: edification.

How to Hear a Prophet

When someone comes to us with a word they think is specifically for us from God, we're invited to hear God in a unique way. Because of counterfeits, though, that word must be tested, and because of our own confusion, it must be applied properly. But if we lose what prophecy can be—a confirming voice, as one word of many words, as one counselor of many counselors—we lose something special from the Holy Spirit.

Prophecy, like teaching, is a Holy Spirit gift that's fallible. It must always be measured by the Word of God and tested against it. Like teaching, prophecy can be delivered in the wrong spirit. We must be loving and committed to the encouragement of the body of Christ. The Holy Spirit will not move your mouth; you must move your mouth. Simply put, you are in control of whether you're going to encourage someone as the Holy Spirit prompts you. That's all prophecy is.

As you grow in your ability to prophetically encourage people, recognizing when the Holy Spirit is prompting you to speak and leading you in your encouragement, you may begin to receive knowledge from the Holy Spirit that is profound wisdom for people: Knowledge such as insights into particular situations you had no clue about, certain words or phrases you employ, or passages of

Scripture that are exactly what that person needed to hear. Or maybe the timing of the encouragement is precisely when that person is ready to receive it to its fullest.

The gift and the giver grow together. The result is a church so Spirit-encouraging and committed to drawing out the God-dreams and destiny in people's lives that hurtful or unbiblical thoughts and attitudes have nowhere to hide and thrive. A church with this type of atmosphere of faith and love and hope can't help but have a strong sense of identity (its destination always and in all circumstances) and be knit together by the bond of peace.

Here's the point: there's a way to receive prophecy and a way not to. Just as we need to learn to prophesy well, we need to learn to receive prophecy well.

First, as I said earlier, all prophecy is to be judged. Just because someone has what feels like a prophetic word to them doesn't mean it's from God. Whenever I get a prophetic encouragement from someone and it doesn't immediately resonate with me, I call a trusted friend or mentor or discuss it with my wife, and ask, "What do you think of this word? Am I not seeing something about myself? Do you think this is God's word to me right now?"

I don't always see things about myself, because, like you, I walk around in denial most of the time. I've learned, however, not to immediately write off any prophetic word but rather to submit prophetic words for judgment. Some prophetic words I've received didn't make sense at first. My dad told me to "sit on it" and see if those words matured over time (or rather, if *I* matured over time). Many times they did. Prophecy isn't always for right now.

As I mentioned before, prophecy doesn't go against the principles of the Word of God. A prophecy is measured by the Word of God. God isn't going to prophetically tell you your pastor is wrong and you're right, so you should call him up and tell him what a doink he is. God isn't going to tell you in a prophetic utterance that you should leave your spouse and marry a famous person. Just like prophecy is by definition communal, its interpretation is communal too.

Sometimes we ignore facts because the facts don't validate our feelings. Therefore, we cannot be the sole interpreters of prophetic words, and this is also why prophecy gets so needlessly weird. Receive a prophetic word with an awareness that people prophesy in part, but that it's okay because we preach and teach in part as well. When a prophetic word has been measured and people you trust have confirmed that it's probably God speaking, treat that prophetic word like it's God speaking! Write it down, memorize it, pray about it, thank God for it, and use it as a tool to wage war.

Second, wage war with what you hear! Oh yeah. You didn't know you're supposed to wage war with your prophetic word? Check this out:

> Timothy, my son, I am giving you this command in keeping with the prophecies once made about you, so that by recalling them you may fight the battle well, holding on to faith and a good conscience, which some have rejected and so have suffered shipwreck with regard to the faith. (1 Timothy 1:18–19, NIV)

What an incredible couple of verses. Paul told Timothy that the difference between Timothy and other guys who had made shipwreck of their faith was that Timothy would pay attention to the specific prophetic words spoken over him.

Prophecy should remind you of who you are. That's why it's so powerful when shared in community. The Bible says there is safety in a "multitude of counselors" (Proverbs 11:14, NKJV). That's okay. Discernment is vital. And *discern* doesn't mean "despise." You can critically evaluate something without writing it off. People who despise prophecy and their prophetic words are disobedient to God and His Word.

God speaks to people clearly through prophecy, and nothing is more life-giving than receiving a prophecy that is clearly *God*. But sometimes people misinterpret what's said, the same way we could be told it's going to rain tomorrow and buy a ticket to Phoenix instead of just finding an umbrella. Our response is in our court. The message is in His.

Maybe we fall into this temptation because we're frustrated with where we are in life or are itching for a change. Ants in the pants, you know? But when we lack maturity, we let our fears and desires shape what we hear, letting through only what we want to hear, what confirms our opinion or plan. If we already want to go, then no matter what God says, we'll hear "Go." If everything in us is screaming to stay, we'll want to stay. Then when what we want to happen doesn't work out, we blame God, doubting what He told us.

Doesn't this highlight the power of a prophetic word? We're reminded that we're not alone in this process of listening. We're hearing Him through the community He's gathering. It's hard to describe the power of this unless you've felt that power for yourself, but it makes this point: *we're not in this thing alone.*

Our job, as always, is the same. To listen and to grow. God *will* lead us and guide us. We are called to be people of the Spirit and people of the Word, but what if both of those calls are just saying we need to be people of the Voice?

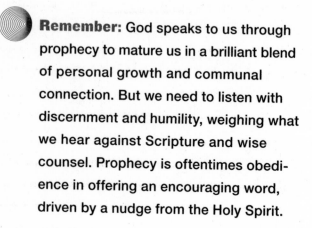

Remember: God speaks to us through prophecy to mature us in a brilliant blend of personal growth and communal connection. But we need to listen with discernment and humility, weighing what we hear against Scripture and wise counsel. Prophecy is oftentimes obedience in offering an encouraging word, driven by a nudge from the Holy Spirit.

CHAPTER SEVEN

The Myth of Disposable Nature

Take a Deep Breath of General Revelation, Baby

If you take a walk outside, are you walking through a message from God? As you look at the incredible intricacy of creation surrounding us in the natural world, do you think this is one way God is talking to His kids?

Odds are this never crosses your mind. Sure, you might see creation as revealing His glory in some vague way, but that's about it. Today creation is seen more like something to be used, something we're in "dominion" over. And the promise of a new earth basically means whatever happens with this one doesn't matter.

With all that in mind, is it just me, or do some Christians have the worst attitudes about nature? Hey, even if you happen to believe *it's all gonna burn,* does that mean you should throw your trash out in creation's face? Do you think God doesn't care about your stewardship of the good things He's made? (And honestly, "new earth" might mean something different from what you think it does.)

You might not think that much of the granola-flavored folks (driving around in the converted-to-biodiesel VWs with the "Tree Hugging Dirt Worshipper" stickers on the bumpers) who over-venerate nature. Respecting nature can be synonymous with automatically becoming some weirdo hippie universalist who hasn't showered in a year and mutters breathily that "shampoo strips your natural oils."

A negative attitude toward creation is exactly why many of us can't hear God speaking through it. After all, we see only what we can see. We hear what we have a category for when it comes to hearing. Why would we even attempt to find any meaning in something we consider a glorified trash bin, to be dominated and used?

That attitude is overtly, expressly, no-doubt-about-it unbiblical.

The Bible's vision of God's creation is of people being integrated into a web of goodness that all reflects God's glory and power. We're called to serve and steward. In no way does *dominion* mean "disconnection" or "abuse." Disposable nature is a myth. And if we believe it, we lose one of the most constant and beautiful ways God speaks to His kids. In fact, we've lost out on one of the great gifts from God: rest, which leads to renewal. You see, our theology of nature is connected to our theology of rest. Rest is holy and integrated with our lives in a flourishing physical world. God blessed humanity, all creation, and the Sabbath—and we lose if we don't encounter His presence in all three.

God speaks through creation—albeit in a slightly different way than more direct means that we hear His voice. One of the most practical and primary ways we can listen for Him is by practicing the spiritual discipline of rest, connecting to the goodness of what He speaks through His creation. Let's focus on that call to goodness we find in the natural world. While God's revelation about Himself in nature is way bigger than just taking a break, for most of us this is the place to start. We can begin to unlock how we hear Him speaking quietly in the "things that have been made" (Romans 1:20).

Oh Goodness!

God speaks through nature similarly to how a painter "speaks" through a painting or a musician "speaks" through a composition. When you're looking at something created, it speaks volumes about who made it, and it invites your response.

Even more specifically, perhaps we can think of nature as something *intended* to reveal things about God, just as if I wrote a song for Jasmine—even if it was instrumental and totally "wordless." It would still communicate something special and vibrant about our relationship.

The Bible talks about all creation revealing the glory of God to all humanity. This is "general revelation," which tells about God's goodness, power, presence, and closeness to humanity. Just read Romans 1, the Psalms, or the story of Paul on Mars Hill to get a sense of the power and scope of this revelatory act. It's amazing. *Everyone* in the world is faced with the basic truths about God, simply by being alive and in the world He's made.

So how did we become so disconnected from this incredible, worldwide gift? I think it began when we started developing some messed-up theology about the world. Messed up, as in *not biblical*. Messed up, as in *harmful*. Messed up, as in *anti-Christian*. Messed up, as in *thinking about nature as less than good*.

We need to remember that the creation and the Sabbath are called *good*. God called them good.

Do we believe that? Do we experience that? What does that goodness mean for us? Are we encountering that goodness? Besides other powerful reasons, God made creation to soothe us and heal us and speak to us. If we cut ourselves off from that, it's our loss.

But with that said, this good creation is under our curse, not working the way it's supposed to be working. Our sin had global implications. The problem with the world isn't God; the problem is *us*. It's *me*. I have willfully sinned and joined the human family tradition in bringing corruption into His world. Nature is fallen because of our choices.

Nature is still God's creation, and it's still good, even though it's under a curse because of humans constantly bringing sin— exploitation, hatred, greed, waste, selfishness, lust—into the world. We inherit the environment we bring upon ourselves, one that is decaying and longing for total renewal, just like we are.

But beauty and wonder are still to be found in this broken world. Yes, life has suffering. Goodness and danger are rarely far apart. Even glorious Hawaii has volcanoes. But we can still find the beaches and lakes and rivers and mountains and the rest and peace they bring us. We still have days when we're, like, *Wow. That's beautiful.* Much of humanity is suffering, but most of humanity knows some things about life are good and some things about life are wrong. We know how creation should be. Even when we can't see it, we can intuit it. Creation still declares "the glory of God" (Psalm 19:1), even under the curse. God's goodness and greatness are everywhere.

We don't worship the created; we worship the Creator. But we sometimes tend to have some unbiblical attitudes toward what God has designed to be a place of healing and nurture. Maybe we need to rethink our attitudes toward recreation and the outdoors and begin to call rest and God's creation what they are—holy and blessed.

Jesus pointed to nature to show God's provision, reminding us that even Solomon in all his glory wasn't as beautifully clothed as "the lilies of the field" (Matthew 6:28–29). That's incredibly poetic. Saint Francis of Assisi remarked that the life and warmth and light and size of the sun reminded him of God. Okay, I get that. But Jesus even saw the Father's care in His detailed concern for grass and sparrows and lilies. Every part of nature can speak to us with the Creator's voice.

Remember that Jesus is the ultimate human—God who came down to show us how to be human. Jesus made these micro observations to show us how. The Christian life isn't emotional or intellectual detachment from the senses; we're called to live fully sensory lives and to experience God in the senses. I think in some ways our frequent dislike of nature comes from an unchristian disgust for the senses in general. The senses are things to be suppressed; if we're enjoying something, we think we're doing something wrong. *Why?*

I think we don't enjoy things enough. Chesterton mused that materialists rarely enjoy their stuff—they just accumulate it for status or to create a sense of security.[13] The way to be thankful for something is to encounter it! The way to discover God in nature again is to find Him at the beach again. Not just to think about it but also to experience it.

In disconnecting from nature, we disconnect from our ability to hear God in what He has made. We must reconnect with that part of ourselves and our faith. Our senses that would discover God's voice in the world have become dulled through both our suspicion and life's pace. We live in the age of progress; we think our society is going forward because technology is going forward. Because faster and easier and more efficient products keep coming to market, helping us to live more efficient and convenient lives, everybody assumes that their interior worlds are progressing and that society somehow must be progressing.

Our phones are faster, our social connectedness is increasing, our planes are faster, our televisions are bigger, and our streaming accounts have more options. It's easier to get ahold of my parents now; I can FaceTime my sister to see Georgie, her baby; and I can google a Scripture verse on my iPhone. Surely if I can reach my parents and Georgie and the Bible that quickly, I can get ahold of God, right? His voice is just a Google search away, right? Why would I need to slow down and take a walk in nature? Speeding up gets me places and gets things done. Slowing down is just that, *slowing down*.

But think about that. Is it so bad?

Restoration, Not Retreat

Hearing God's voice may require you to go back to the ABCs of life. Getting back to what's real is usually about getting back to the basics. Are you feeling worn out and tired? You probably need a week of sleeping on a beach or sitting quietly in your home with a good book. Rest is holy. It's not laziness; it's restoration.

We tend to think that a retreat into nature is a retreat from life. We think that going to the lake and sitting on the deck as we watch the sunset over the water is a royal waste of time. And in a sense, it is. But that's exactly what it's supposed to be. Simply going for a nature walk isn't the idea here. God's voice comes to those who purposefully and regularly withdraw from an obsession with self-sufficiency and striving into a place of physical and emotional rest in God.

Jesus, the light and life of the world, retreated into nature often and alone. Jesus practiced "Sabbath" throughout His life and ministry. He regularly withdrew from the work of the ministry—away from the crowds and even away from His disciples—to "Sabbath" and receive from the Father.

A busy, anxious soul can look at nature and hear absolutely nothing because it's so flummoxed by the goings-on of life. A Sabbath soul can look at nature and notice that God is at work in the grass.

Sabbath is the discipline of intentionally resting in God, the laying down of one's tools. It's a recognition that our ability has limits, but there is no limit to God's ability. It's trusting that God can make up for our "loss of working time" while we withdraw into rest with Him. It's voluntarily recognizing that God oversees outcomes. Sabbath is a shedding of self-reliance and a fixing of our gaze on the One from whom all life flows.

The Bible is full of stories of men and women who heard

God's voice in the retreats of life, when they abandoned the hustle of their own empire building for a season of rest and solitude in God. Paul the apostle spent fourteen years in retreat and received incredible apostolic revelation (Galatians 1:17). From the Isle of Patmos, John saw heaven (Revelation 1:9–11). John the Baptist was a wilderness dweller (Matthew 3:1). God appeared to Moses in the wilderness (Exodus 3:1). The Holy Spirit fell upon the early church in the upper room as they waited on God (Acts 2:1–3). The Holy Spirit spoke prophetically to Paul (then Saul) and Barnabas about their ministry as they were fasting and worshipping (Acts 13:1–2). But nature is everywhere. In the suburbs. In the cities. You just have to look for it.

Jonathan Edwards often retreated to a certain tree for prayer and reflection, and on several occasions he had an ecstatic charismatic encounter with the Holy Spirit. He lay on the grass, weeping for hours, filled with the power of God and completely overcome by the love of God. Edwards noted that he hadn't retreated to this quiet spot in nature for anything but to read and pray (he wasn't looking for an experience), but those experiences happened as he practiced the discipline of withdrawal and rest and Sabbath. God's voice came to him repeatedly in that discipline, not just from reading and prayer but also in transformational encounter.[14]

C. S. Lewis once remarked that, if we're driving along a road and we've missed our turn, progress is turning around and going back to the road we're supposed to go down.[15] Our souls and our society have a challenging time with this idea, because we never think of progress as a going back but almost always as a going forward. It all becomes much more complicated when we think our lives are naturally progressing (we think this because we're caught up in the age of technological progress) and when we use metrics such as money and comfortability or even the progress of society as spiritual markers.

Decluttering the Heart

What do you do when you're trying to talk on your phone with too much noise in the background? You go to a quiet place. Someplace where distractions and background noise are minimized. You *don't* walk into the middle of Times Square. You *don't* crank up the stereo. You *don't* walk into a crowded coffee shop and start shouting "Can you hear me now?" into your phone.

Quiet *really* helps us hear. But to tell you the truth, the noise I bring with me is often the real issue. You know what I mean?

My first couple of days away from the busyness of life are usually filled with *panic*. I'm still reaching for my phone the same time I'm trying to come down from the frenzy and hustle I've whipped myself into. I've also noticed that my breaks are too far apart; I'm not resting enough. It shouldn't take me so long to let go of the absurd idea that life will fall apart if I'm not at my desk. My soul needs the lull of the ocean waves, with my stupid phone off; my mind needs to hear the wind through the palm trees.

My soul is so broken and supercharged by life that it takes me a week to relax when I go on vacation. Have you ever been on a vacation and noticed that by the end of it you're just starting to feel relaxed and soothed?

God calls us into nature and rest to remind us that He's in control of the world. We tend to think that we're in control of our provision, of others, of our lives—maybe even the sun. Of just too much. The point of Sabbath in the Old Testament is to remind our panicked souls that the Lord is our Shepherd. We don't make the sun come up or go down. We don't make the ocean roar or calm. We don't decide if the mountains are snowcapped. God is God. He makes things grow. He sends the rain and the snow and controls the sun. He makes our world habitable.

When our lives are busy and cluttered and fast paced and noisy, and we begin to become irritated and on edge and distracted, our spirits start to suffer and starve. We are spirit, soul, and body, each distinguishable but interconnected. The health of your body affects the health of your soul (mind, emotions, desire); an unhealthy body and unhealthy soul drag on the spirit.

Psalm 131:2–3 says, "I have calmed and quieted myself, I am like a weaned child with its mother. . . . Israel, put your hope in the LORD" (NIV). The psalmist has performed a physical action, and his soul has stilled. Now his spirit has connected to its Creator, and the entirety of his personhood is aligned in a trusting hope. Spiritual order begins with physical order.

Your body matters to God because it's connected to your soul and spirit. If the body didn't matter, God wouldn't redeem it in the Resurrection. Neither would He send His Spirit to indwell it right now. Many spiritual problems are woven together with physical problems. Not sleeping affects your relationship with God. Overwork affects your relationship with God. Sins of the body (illicit sexual acts, alcoholism, drug abuse, and so on) affect your relationship with God. Our thoughts and emotions stir into chaos because of the state of the body.

This means losing touch with our bodies, and our "very good" connection with the physical world affects everything. And because our bodies aren't disconnected from the rest of us, that makes it hard to hear God in *every* area. But if that's true, then the *opposite* must be true as well: the body and the world of creation can powerfully connect us relationally with God and to hear His voice.

This is all tied in with rest. God wants us to work, to create and cultivate and produce, and to repair and learn and develop, because this good work is one of the reasons God made us humans. We reflect Him in our good work. God makes things, and it's good for us to work in imitation of Him.

Withdrawal from our man-made projects and into the rest of the natural world is holy. The beach is holy. The woods are too. So are the mountains, urban parks, gardens, and the outback, and *anywhere* we encounter the rawness and simple goodness of God's general revelation. These places are the edge of striving and the beginning of trust—*if* we're willing to let go of what we cling to and meet God there. If we encounter them rightly, we bring nothing to these places and that's part of how and why we hear God in nature.

But have we understood the ways God intends for us to encounter revelation when we encounter His rest? I don't think we have. I haven't, at least. We've run ourselves ragged, and we've lost our minds trying to keep going without God's rest. Now our spirits are in continual crisis mode. That's a terrible place, a place of distraction and burnout. Have you ever tried to have an important conversation when you could barely keep your eyelids open? The person you're talking to usually says, "We'll talk later. Go get a nap."

I wonder how clear God's voice would become if we took more vacation time. Honestly. I wonder how clear God's voice would become if we developed a relaxing hobby that we took seriously. Maybe that breakthrough idea for our work is on the other side of two weeks at the lake with the fam. Maybe that inspiration, that breakthrough, is on the other side of a month of good sleep, coupled with sunset drives and a home-cooked dinner.

Maybe it's time to declutter. God wants to get the idea of His incredible care and powerful provision into your heart, but there's no room in there. What if you removed the distractions that can send you into a panic attack and dealt with the root of the problem?

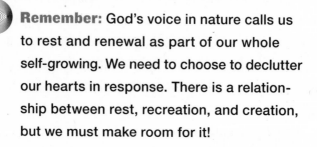

Remember: God's voice in nature calls us to rest and renewal as part of our whole self-growing. We need to choose to declutter our hearts in response. There is a relationship between rest, recreation, and creation, but we must make room for it!

CHAPTER EIGHT

The Myth of Greener Grasses

Maybe God Is Talking Through Your Dead-End Job or Other Less-Than-Ideal Circumstances (Additionally, I Worry Somewhat That I'm Making These Chapter Subtitles Too Long. Thoughts, Dear Reader?)

I was recently with a friend when he had to break some news to his five-year-old son, Alexander. They were moving across the country. Ever helpful, I joined in. "You're going to be close to Disneyland!" I shouted. "Remember Disneyland? You *love* Disneyland! And there's no *winter* in California like there is in New York, so you can go outside and play all year round! And you'll live near the beach, and you love the beach! And it's warm there . . ."

As I droned on with my starry-eyed California dreamin', the boy just sort of stared—first out the window, then at his shoes, then at the ceiling of the truck we were driving in. I could tell he couldn't process any of it. I could see the wheels turning: *Moving? What* is *moving? What is time? What is permanence?* After about a minute, his dad broke the silence. "What do you think, buddy?" Alexander furrowed his brow, then asked, "Will I still be able to see Johnny?"

Johnny is his best buddy from school. They do everything together. Soccer team, swimming lessons, trips to the playground—all of kindergarten life. Johnny, in Alexander's eyes, is basically his *world*.

How different that perspective is from, say, his dad's take on the move. Big adult brains evaluate life on a totally different playing field. We're looking past what we think is the impermanence of kindergarten friendships (not that they aren't *important,* but they're generally not what we base life decisions on). We tried to make the move appealing to Alexander with much larger concepts—what we think makes life good for him—but he couldn't wrap his head around it. Even with Disneyland involved.

Our little visions and conceptions of life can handle only so much. We aren't ready to hear everything God has for us when we're asking the equivalent of whether our best friend, Johnny, is going to be there. We can't comprehend His goodness yet, because our character and creativity are still in the process of expansion. Our feelings matter, but we can't see the whole picture. What a powerful image of how we interpret our circumstances according to what matters most to us.

One way God speaks to His children is through circumstances. Along with so many other means of communication, the events, opportunities, and setbacks of our lives are powerful ways we can learn about God's character and desires for us. These circumstances can be as simple as a "random" meeting with a friend. They can be as complex as the talents He gives us. All of them matter, but we need to embrace them with a healthy perspective.

You see, many of us become fixated on what we think we need rather than allowing the possibility of a larger perspective than our own. I have all the sympathies in the world for all us little Alexanders, but sometimes we become so committed to trying to make everything work out our way that we miss the very way that God has already spoken and shaped us for maturity through our unique circumstances. We believe, all too easily, the myth that the grasses are greener in pastures where the Shepherd hasn't led us.

I spent almost five years studying at Bible college, from the age of nineteen to twenty-four. (The extra year was necessary because I was kicked out several semesters for being an idiot—most deservedly, because I was one.) Many types of people go to Bible college. Some want to be in "vocational" ministry (of my graduating class, maybe ten of us work in full-time ministry now). Some are sent to Bible college as a punitive measure or a stand-in for a rehab program (we had tons of these, generally guys). Others "want to take a year of my life and study the Word." And some (I think deep down this was everyone) want to find out what God wants for their lives. I can't say I met many guys and girls who had a singular vision for their lives when entering Bible college.

People with clear vision seemed like the exception. The rule was that none of us had a clue.

That question (*What does God want from me?*) haunted us. The answer is what we listened for as we sat in our lectures; it was what we dreamed about in our tiny dorm rooms. We all wanted to experience an audible voice, telling us why we were born and what we were going to do.

Sometimes it got a little strange. Some students made pronouncements about who they were going to marry. And of course, without fail, every year multiple guys went up to girls at our Bible college and made total fools of themselves by telling them about their great prophetic destiny together, as allegedly revealed by the third person of the holy Trinity.

When we constantly overemphasize ecstatic experience and highly unique circumstances as "spiritual," highly anxious young people begin to abandon wisdom living and go on that God's Voice Safari that inevitably ends with disappointment and more confusion.

Pomp and Circumstances

Let's look through one lens to begin: the lens of our work. One of the questions wisdom asks of somebody trying to find out "what God is telling them to do" is "What gifts or skills or abilities has God given you?" In our circumstances—including our inner circumstances, such as talent, gifting, and opportunity—God speaks to us implicitly. Being incredible at music doesn't *have* to mean you're called to be a musician, but it sure means God is asking you to consider it carefully. It could be that God is saying, *Hey, I gave you this gift, and you're passionate about it! You've been incredibly faithful with it, and now it's blossomed and become something wonderful. I want to use this to speak to and minister to your neighbor and your church!*

Because for many people the focus on God's voice can be external (especially through circumstances), people miss what He's saying through what He has done and is doing internally. You don't need a prophetic word to do what God has already put inside your heart!

I think there's a lot of confusion about vocation and calling. Many of us think kingdom work is opposed to "secular" work. Yes, the kingdom of God is different from the kingdoms of this world, but *secular* is not the right word to assign to the world God created and loves.

Your job at a shoe store doesn't need justifying; you don't need to explain how you're redeeming that place by working there. To love your neighbor and quietly "work with your hands" (1 Thessalonians 4:11) is good enough. God cares about these things, and the kingdom of shoes is not at odds with the kingdom of God. One day the kingdoms of this world will have become the kingdom of our God, but until then God isn't trying to pull people out of the shoe business and make them all evangelists or pastors. Selling shoes doesn't need to be a ministry, either. You don't need to spiritualize or justify the redemptive value of your job.

The issue here is that we're all so anxious, thinking we're not doing what God wants us to do because we think we haven't "heard" Him correctly. All these superspiritual people are hearing audible voices and experiencing "divine appointments" and "God shifts" and "Holy Spirit leading," and you're stuck at the mall wondering if God has forgotten about you while you're doing the devil's work.

No, you're doing work that matters to God. Believe it or not, God provided that job for you, and you're right where you're supposed to be. What's probably giving you anxiety is that you're mistaking vocation for calling.

You are called to follow Jesus. That's your primary calling. After that, there's a multiplicity of callings on your life. Your calling isn't just a job. If you're married, you're called to be a loving, supporting spouse. If you're a son or daughter, you're called to be a loving, supportive child to your parents. You're called to disciple

(Matthew 28); you're called to be a part of a local church (Acts 2); you're called to "love your neighbor as yourself" (Matthew 22:39); and you're called to lay hold of that for which Christ Jesus laid hold of you (Philippians 3:12, NKJV). Your callings can also totally switch, even multiple times in life! You may not even discover a huge calling on your life until you're older! Bill Gates believes his calling is to give away money. He didn't realize that until he was in his fifties![16]

Most of us think that all the little bits of our lives (the years we worked at McDonald's, our paper route, our crummy college-era jobs, the little skills we have, the big skills we have, our relationships, our gifts and talents and strengths of character and personality) are all throwaway bits because one day God is going to tell us to do something more important that has nothing to do with our past.

But God has a way of crafting our lives into these beautiful mosaics, pieced together with all the different cuts and colors of our stories. For most of us, our call goes through all kinds of activity and inactivity, vocation and unvocation, employment and unemployment. As with an unfinished puzzle, we're impatiently wanting the picture to be clearer. But as we continue to be faithful with what He's given us—what is already in our hands to do—the puzzle begins to have more fitted pieces, and the picture does become clearer.

We must resist the temptation to put too much strain on our various jobs and vocations, as if they're supposed to be these sacred, all-satisfying endeavors, rather than understanding that we have a multiplicity of callings. Things change. We grow.

What gifts do you have? What gets you excited? What do people say you're good at? Ephesians 4:7 says each of us has been given a measure of grace. Romans 12:3 says each of us has a measure of faith. Ephesians 4:11 (NIV) talks about how God gave some to be apostles, prophets, evangelists, pastors, and teachers. In 1 Corinthians 15:10, Paul said, "By the grace of God . . . I worked." God has given you some grace-ability, and He's given you some faith, and that's His way of saying, *This is what I want you to do.*

Could it be that God is speaking to you *right now* through the abilities and opportunities He's given you? If so, what would it mean for you to listen?

Ants in the Pants

"But why am I not functioning in this gifting or that gifting? I feel like I'm stuck at a dead-end job and that my real passion and skill have fallen by the wayside! God is so silent!"

God speaks and works in seasons (He invented and ordained our four seasons, and He called them good—yes, even winter). God also speaks through the different times and circumstances in our lives, which we often call seasons as well. Problem is, we want to be in a season of harvest like the dude you follow online, all tan and fruitful and flourishing, but God's going, *Yeah, I need you to be in a winter season right now.*

During winter, the sap in a tree reverses and goes down into the roots to nourish and grow the core of the tree. Because of this sap reversal, the boughs of the tree begin to lose their vegetation and signs of life; they soon become bare without a single external indication of the past summer. They look ugly and dead. But internally the tree has never been more alive. Its roots are growing, it's becoming more secure and permanent as a local fixture, its roots are discovering more water and moisture, and it's becoming ready to sustain the growth and fruit the coming summer will bring it.

Many of us, especially if we're younger and in college, have jobs that are prevocational: they're helping us pay for the training we're receiving for our vocation. But for years after college, we can still be preparing, not functioning in work we thought we'd finally be functioning in. We're still in that prevocational season (or perhaps even a postvocational season—maybe we weren't ready, or the job market dried up), and if we don't realize what season we're in (a season of preparation; a season of repreparation), we'll be so confused about what God is thinking and doing and ultimately saying through it all!

See, here's the thing: you can walk out a door, but you can't walk out of a season. Stop looking for an exit; come to terms with your season. Once you know what season you're in, you suddenly have context for what God is saying. If you're in a winter season, it's time to focus on health, on root systems, and on all the things God is emphasizing and highlighting. That's what He will be speaking to you about. Once you've identified that season, watch at how loud and focused God's speech will become. You'll start to notice all the ways He was trying to communicate with you, but you couldn't hear Him because you were focused on summer words and themes and motifs.

God speaks through opportunities. But here's the trick: not

all opportunities are from God, even though He uses them as confirmation in our lives.

The reality is that mine is the ants-in-the-pants generation—we can't sit still. We can't do anything for longer than five seconds. We can't look one another in the eyes. We can't finish reading a book. We can't hold a thought. We can't wait for what's next. We don't need much of an opportunity to sprint through the door!

The door that looks so good could be the worst opportunity ever, but because we're so antsy in the ole pantsy, we bolt! We give no time to assessing why we're where we are in the present, and we don't engage in a process of submitting opportunities to others in our lives who aren't emotionally drunk on the possibility of what's next. (Most of us are so antsy that we hardly even have these types of relationships; they take too long to build, and you have to be in the same place for too long to build them. Real relationship is built through frequency and proximity, two things hard to have when you've got those ants!) We just walk through the first opportunity that presents itself.

When I was about thirteen (when my dad began to realize I had talent as a musician), Dad told me someone would always be asking me to go somewhere because of my gift. Sure enough, he was right. I was asked to play nearly everywhere by almost everyone I knew. In Bible college I was asked to plant churches. I was offered staff positions. I was offered jobs. I've been offered churches to pastor. And I wonder how miserable I would have been had I been dumb enough to say yes to some of those offers. Thankfully I had people in my life who shut them down and talked me off a ledge.

The opportunities were absolutely confirming something that

it took me years to see—that I should be faithful with the gifts God has given me. I never wanted to be in ministry, because I didn't think I fit the mold. But God had other plans. What was needed was for me to change my idea of what those roles meant. *I* was called. I could still be me.

You aren't in charge of promotion—that comes from the Lord. But you are responsible to go deep in the winter, sow in the spring, rest in the summer, and harvest in the fall. You're responsible for recognizing that life has seasons and that faithfulness looks like responding appropriately in each one.

People who refuse to recognize seasons and live their lives only going through doors are like tall trees that never develop root systems. They don't go deep enough to support themselves on their own. They must lean on something else or fall flat. Why? Because they haven't been challenged enough. They've never submitted themselves to God's winter season, where He speaks to issues of depth of character and purpose. They have no context to hear that. They've always had a door because they've always had a little bit of talent. Their unguarded "strength" has become a double weakness; the talent meant to be developed and deepened and matured and patiently refined has become a cheap subway trick that gets them pennies. They will eventually collapse under the weight of their own so-called success.

A trend in my generation is to travel, to "learn more about the world," with an accompanying belief that the more traveling you've done, that the more transient your life is, you're somehow a more cultured, well-rounded, self-actualized person. In his book

Heretics, G. K. Chesterton takes issue with Rudyard Kipling, the father of all modern wanderlust, a rootless English gentleman living in India and writing critiques of England and British culture. Chesterton, a proud Englishman, critiques Kipling profoundly, explaining that it is precisely within our daily grind, more specifically within the context of our immediate family and neighbors, that our souls expand and become larger. Kipling called the Englishman living in the countryside "small minded"; Chesterton argued that Kipling knew England "as an intelligent Englishman knows Venice."[17]

The soul doesn't expand because you've seen old castles; it expands because you've been forced to endure Grandpa's politics at the dinner table. The soul expands because you've had no other option but to make up with your brothers and sisters, year after year; because you've had to learn how to plead your case before your mother, who serves as judge, jury, and executioner; because your father held your feet to the fire when you wanted to give up and taught you the weight of your words and commitments; because your house was small and you had to share the space, inventing ways to make-believe you were somewhere else, hollowing out metacognitive space in which to dwell. "With fairyland opening at the gate, is the man with large ideas. His mind creates distance; the motor-car stupidly destroys it."[18]

Chesterton admits that the greatest outcome of travel is to come back to your home and see it in a new light. But simply seeing new terrain and customs isn't how travel expands the soul—it must be endured, like your homelife and the seventh grade are endured. Soul expansion is about so much more than experience. It's about rootedness.

God doesn't mature you by traveling you; He matures you by planting you. Dead things travel a lot. They're called tumbleweeds. Rootless.

This doesn't mean God won't tell you to go somewhere. We're talking about the maturing and leading voice of God here. One of God's vital seasons is the planting season of life, when your roots go down. He won't uproot you just to make you rootless. God's voice is a wise Father voice—He wants you to be continually fruitful (remember, you're fruitful even in the winter because roots are growing!), so He will speak in the season and use doors to confirm His grace and potential opportunity. Then when the timing is right, He'll begin to present doors you may want to walk through.

Once, when I was frustrated with God in a season of my life, I turned to my friend Joel and started complaining about my lack of opportunity. Joel said he believed that God wanted to plant me and anchor me, but my ants-in-the-pants mentality was working against me. He said, "It's like every time God's about to bring you blessing, you uproot yourself and run in a different direction."

He was right.

I was running way out in front of God's voice, and because I thought every door of opportunity *was* His voice, I just kept walking through the doors. But they took me further and further away from the need of and inevitability of the maturing that comes with planting.

How are your roots doing, friend? Are you running away from the place you need to be *stuck* for a while?

When God Says "Go"

One of my profs at Bible college, Ken Malmin, told us, "If God calls you to leave somewhere, it should *hurt*. Because if you've let your roots go down deep and you've been faithful to focus on your season and on what God has commissioned you to do in that place, it will be in some ways a painful process of lifting up your root systems and moving them elsewhere."

Many of us have that last-day-at-work fantasy, typically while we're showering, when we have that final heated exchange with our boss, letting him (or her) know what we really think. (I've found that the shower is where I'm planning and winning all my future arguments.) You've kept it in all this time, waiting to get out of there, hating your job, and now you're going to be free. Now you're going to be vindicated by God Himself, because He's opened a door of opportunity and all your problems and restrictions are going to be gone. Fly, blackbird, fly.

But that's not how calling works.

God's voice in a season change or in a door of opportunity shouldn't necessarily be a complete surprise either. As you've been faithful, you've been growing and dreaming and thinking and aware of your strengths. These things aren't to be ignored but tempered and submitted to people who love you and care for you.

But God's voice in a season change or in a door of opportunity should come as somewhat of a surprise. God put Adam into a deep sleep while He was creating the best possible gift for him—Eve. I tend to think God prefers this mode—when we're settled and in a place of obedience, yielded to the processes of life, and then awake to incredible things He's been weaving out of our very sides, undetected.

Storms and Worms

God even speaks through storms. Think about the story of Jonah! Circumstances rocked him every step of the way, but he didn't repent, despite storms . . . and worms.

God will send storms to move you. He'll send fish to spit you up onto the place you're supposed to be, and then He'll create a shade tree to comfort you through the storm process. Next He'll send a worm to move you out of your comfortability again and into your calling. We curse storms and worms; we think they're all from the Enemy. But God is in control of the weather. I mean, that's biblical. Jesus pulled that trick out of His sleeve a couple of times, and God sends worms to move us from indecision and immobility and into the thick of life.

Maybe you're cursing what God is blessing. Maybe you prayed that dangerous prayer, *God, speak to me about my* _____. *Help me, Lord.* And God is answering your prayer by taking away every other option so you can't just delay obedience and divert your attention and energy from what you're called to do!

Maybe the storms and worms in your life are God trying to get your attention and tell you you're headed in the wrong direction! You've been asking Him to confirm your dream, but your dream isn't the God-dream. Maybe God's using the storm not just to get you out of the boat but also to get you into a different boat altogether.

If you're in the middle of a stormy circumstance, maybe you need to ask, *Father, is this You? Are You wanting to move me along? Or are You checking the foundations of my house, to see if I've built it on the Rock?* Not every storm is from God! Sometimes we rock the boat just fine by ourselves!

God speaks through circumstances, but not every circumstance is God speaking. Not every worm is a prophet. But maybe every prophet needs a worm. They keep the people of God remembering what's important.

We must yield to the wisdom processes of life when we're trying to discern God's voice in circumstance. Life is developmental; it requires patience. We lack patience and we lack wisdom. Read James chapter 1. It's as if James is writing to a bunch of people who are trying to discern God's voice, just like we are.

God is in the business of training up sons and daughters, and He uses life to shape us and train us. We don't have to be tossed to and fro by the circumstances of life, but He's also using those circumstances to speak.

As we are matured by the seasons of life—as we yield patiently to these processes of working seemingly dead-end jobs, of collaborating with highly irritating people, of taking discipline on the chin for being tardy, of not cheating the system or others but working our way up through the ranks honestly and ethically—we begin to discover what we're made of. We start to settle into our skin, so to speak. We don't get panicky in the seasons but rather learn the God-ordained rhythms of life. And as patience has had its perfect work, and we allow the seasons to have their perfect work, doors of opportunity begin to present themselves, and the wisdom (and self-awareness) we've accumulated through the seasons helps us navigate life.

Sometimes I wonder if God's more into shaping us with His voice than He's into telling us what to do. I see Him watching over you with a giant bucket of theater popcorn, wondering what you're going to do next, pleased that you're discovering the gold He's placed inside of you and allowing the seasons to refine it. He's looking at these doors of opportunity that have come to you, excited to see which one you choose.

 Remember: God speaks to us through the big and little circumstances of our lives. Whether we can hear Him depends on how willing we are to embrace where we are right now.

CHAPTER NINE

The Myth of Solid Water

What Does It Take to Step Out of the Boat?

Peter answered him, "Lord, if it is you,
command me to come to you on the water."

—Matthew 14:28

Walking on water and moving mountains are the two great New Testament signposts of faith preachers most often point to. The idea is that biblical faith can operate in otherwise impossible ways and remove impossible barriers. I wholeheartedly agree.

And I *maaaaay* have tried it out.

Enter Nathan Finochio, age twelve.

On a muggy summer afternoon somewhere in Northern Ontario, I was standing on the dock of a small lake, staring at the surface of the water, wondering if I could muster the same type of faith Peter had and repeat the miracle he experienced. I sat down on the edge of the dock and, resting one foot atop the surface of the shallows, I wondered if my faith could at least support one of my skinny little legs. A rush of faith, a little weight on the leg.

My foot sank right through.

All right, maybe I need to just go all-in, to really *put my faith and hope and trust in God and not do any of this half-hearted stuff.*

Full of the most buoyant kind of trust, I ran off the dock as fast as I could. For a split second, as my feet touched the water, I felt joy surge through me. Then I got a face full of water, sinking like a stone until I swam back up to the surface, sputtering.

I swam back to the dock, wondering why my faith hadn't worked. I supposed I hadn't believed hard enough. I mean, that's how faith works. Right? You just *believe* hard enough?

Is that it?

Fast-forward to college, where funnily enough, a prof told our class about his doing the exact same thing. He recounted his detailed inner dialogue as he stepped out onto a lake, off a dock, with a predictable outcome. The class erupted with laughter. I laughed externally, but internally I was ticked. I was angry that no one had ever explained why faith is so confusing. If it's so essential to Christianity and important to God, why doesn't it work? Or more precisely, why didn't I understand it?

Faith as a By-Product

In this chapter, we turn our attention from means God uses to speak to us, to focus on what His means are supporting—the maturing work of faith. Faith is in a symbiotic relationship with God's voice. They're chicken-and-egg things, as are so many others. God speaks to build our faith. Our faith lets us hear Him.

I think Matthew 14 (in the passage with Peter walking on water) can be understood only in light of Romans 10:17, where Paul explains, "Faith comes from hearing, and hearing through the word of Christ." You see, faith isn't just believing hard, straining until you pop a blood vessel of the soul. Faith is a by-product of hearing God.

Let that sink in for a minute.

Taking a closer look at Matthew 14, we read in verse 22 that Jesus "made the disciples get into the boat and go before him to the other side." The word *made* in Greek is *anankazo,* which means "force," "press," "compel."[19] The disciples got into the boat only because Jesus forcibly told them to do it. Jesus gave them a direct order, and they obeyed Him. They didn't know Jesus had a plan for that evening, and that plan involved a geography and a place and a direction and a storm and a revelation. And an "other side," where a bunch of ministry would take place. My guess is that Jesus also had a big reveal in mind: He was going to show His disciples more of Himself, and this little evening boat trip across a lake in weather that would get stormy was the perfect way to illustrate His point.

But several of the disciples were expert sailors—they knew how boats and bad weather worked together. The Scripture says that by evening there was bad weather, and the boat was already out in the middle of the lake getting pounded by the waves.

The disciples probably pointed at the sky when Jesus was, like, "Hey, guys, jump in, and I'll meet you on the other side." One of the more seasoned fishermen was probably, like, "Are You blind? Also, You're a carpenter. And *that* is a storm front coming *this* way. That means there's a nasty headwind. I'm not getting in that boat!" Jesus had to *press* them to get in the boat. Why? I think it was because He wanted to show them something that needed a storm as its backdrop.

In an act of faith and obedience, they board. As I see it, James is ticked, Peter is terrified, and they're wondering how this can possibly be a good idea.

I was on a plane recently when the turbulence was notably bad. The captain had to ask the flight attendants to take their seats several times because of how much weaving and bobbing we were doing. I fly a lot, but I never really get "over" turbulence, especially when it gets bumpy like that and the plane is dipping.

I know turbulence isn't what makes planes crash; pockets of warm air are just knocking us around. So while it still freaks me out every now and then, in the back of my mind I know that we're going to be fine and that planes are built for this. But I can't even imagine how those guys were feeling. Sinking was a possibility—a very possible possibility. With each big wave came a scream. (Think about this: The Bible records that Peter saw waves that scared him. He was a professional fisherman, but he saw stuff that made him lose it. Those must have been pretty legit waves.)

All the disciples wanted was off that stupid boat and through that storm.

Now, the disciples have been rowing through this storm all night. They're exhausted, and they're still trying to get this boat to the other side. It's the fourth watch of the night—between 3 a.m. and 6 a.m. John chapter 6 records that by this point they have rowed against the wind and waves for three or four miles! These guys are exhausted and tired and scared!

Jesus waits for the perfect time to freak the jibblies out of them. As if this isn't a bad enough situation, Jesus starts to walk toward them, way out on the stormy lake. As He approaches, they begin to panic because they think they see a ghost! The Bible says, "They cried out in fear" because of Jesus's trick (Matthew 14:26). Think of the sound you make when you scare someone half to death. *That's* the kind of cry these guys are letting out when they see Jesus! As if the storm isn't scary enough, now they've got a *ghost* on their hands?

Jesus basically has to call out to them, "Guys, it's just Me. Chill out!"

Peter, always looking for the back door in a sticky situation, cries out, "Lord, if it is you, command me to come to you on the water" (verse 28).

As in, "I will be safe with You, Jesus, and definitely not in this boat. Jesus, You are my exit strategy! Call me, please!"

Jesus says, "Come" (verse 29).

Peter was able to have water-walking faith because Jesus told him to come.

If Jesus hadn't said, "Come," Peter would've sunk like a stone. That's how faith works. We continue what Christ has started, believing despite ourselves.

But the walk didn't last long. Peter, seeing the size of the waves and feeling the strength of the wind, started to sink. The power to walk on the water came from the word from Jesus and the faith that came from hearing Him. When Peter didn't focus on Christ's word, his faith dissipated. Faith is available to us only in response to Jesus. It doesn't come from any other place. How could it?

Splashdown and Substance

Faith isn't a presumption, yet a lot of Christians live "wet" lives. They've tried to copy the faith acts of other people who have heard from God, only to walk off a dock and plunge into situations way out of their depth. Then they blame God, wondering why He isn't working some miraculous provision, eventually just chalking their failure up to "life." The issue? They aren't connected in relational obedience to the God who calls them.

Faith doesn't mean acting on what God *can* do; it's acting on what God has *said* He will do. Making decisions based on what God can do isn't wisdom, and it's certainly not faith. Once again, we need to come back to the clear biblical definition of how faith comes. Of course, "Faith is the assurance of things hoped for, the [evidence] of things not seen" (Hebrews 11:1). But it's certainly not the evidence of things not heard.

Faith comes by hearing. It's as simple as that.

If God hasn't said it, you can't have faith for it. Faith doesn't begin with you; it begins with God. If God *has* said it, you *can* have faith for it! Faith isn't about you; it's about God and His words. This takes all the pressure off you, because it's less about what you can do and more about what you can hear. If you can hear it, you can do it. God does all His creative work by speaking things into existence. We do all our creative work by hustling things into existence. A faith life is less hustling and more hearing. A faith life realizes that God-given faith is powerful and can move mountains and that you don't need a lot of it for incredible things to happen.

We think we need a lot of faith to please God, that we need "great faith" to get biblical things done. But Jesus said size doesn't matter. He said if you have faith even the size of a mustard seed (Matthew 17:20—and that's *tiny*, by the way), you can move mountains. That means a faith life has little to do with what you contribute to it and a lot to do with what God is speaking and saying. The context of Romans 10:17 is saving faith—the type of faith that believes God. If we believe Jesus says who He is and will do what He has said He will do, then we can live a life of faith. It's about trusting the One who's speaking, not your own ability to perfectly believe.

As Peter shifts his belief from what Jesus is saying to what he can see in the wind and the waves, he begins to sink. He cries out, "Lord, save me" (Matthew 14:30). Once again, Peter is putting himself in these situations where he needs saving. I find it interesting that Mark's gospel (which is considered by most scholars to be Peter's gospel, dictated to Mark) doesn't include Peter's walking on water but only Jesus's walking on water and saving the men in the boat. John's gospel does the same thing. The point for Peter and John is that they saw Jesus walk on water and that He saved their lives that day from a terrible storm. For Matthew, Peter's walking on water isn't a triumph, either; it ends with an *almost*.

Sometimes this text is presented as if we're all meant to be walking on water. Let's not forget that Jesus takes Peter back to the boat. Sometimes we preach this text about how we can do impossible things like walk on water if God has called us to. Let's also not forget that this text is about Jesus walking on water and Peter failing. Nobody ever walks on water again. This is more about what God can do and less about what we can do, even though we can respond to what God has said and impossible things can be experienced. Sometimes we preach this text as if *no miracles happened in the boat.*

Eleven miracles happened in the boat—eleven faith miracles. The men were told to be in the boat and stay in the boat. They didn't want to be in that boat; they wanted to be sleeping on dry land, back where the feeding of the multitude had occurred. They wanted to be snuggled up in a dry blanket near a warm fire with some dry bread. Instead, they were soaking wet, sleep deprived, panic stricken, and about to lose their marbles. Here comes Jesus, walking through the storm. They learn that day that He is God. They learn that day that, at His word, they can do impossible things. They learn that day that He has total control over nature.

Jesus doesn't take Peter out for a walk on the water with Him. Jesus grabs Peter and takes him back to the boat. The boat is still where Jesus wants Peter to be; it's still where he wants all of them to be. Once Jesus gets into the boat, the waves and the wind die down, and they all worship Jesus. They're worshipping Him in a new way because they've seen a completely new angle of His divinity. They're worshipping Him because they're grateful to be alive. They're worshipping Him because now He's in the boat with them, and they're going to be all right. The storm was totally worth it.

Faith isn't just about believing for whatever you want; it's about believing God for what He has said. And if we know we've heard Him about something, we can have mountain-moving faith as we believe Him at His word. Often, we hear God's more direct voice in that boat of general obedience. And general obedience shouldn't be considered any less important; it's hard to stay faithful, because we're so jumpy naturally! Those of us living obedient lives to God's general will can know that Jesus is in the boat with us, leading us into incredible destiny with Him, even through the storms of life.

God cares about His words to us. He works through them to bring restoration and healing and hope.

Life in the Boat

Theologians typically categorize God's will for our lives as twofold: God's general will and God's specific will.[20] God's general will is stuff clearly revealed in Scripture: God doesn't want you to murder people; God wants you to be in a church; God wants you to love your neighbor; God wants you to obey your parents.

God's general will is like the boat in Matthew 14. Jesus commanded the disciples to get in the boat. The boat was where they were going to see Jesus in a brand-new way and get to the other side and witness kingdom ministry on the other side. God has a general will boat He wants all of us to get in and stay in. That general will boat is going to take you through storms if you'll stay in it and allow yourself to see Jesus as He truly is. It will also keep you from drowning, making stupid decisions that will ruin your life and force God to intervene. God wants you to be mature and learn wisdom living. Wisdom is how God created the world, and He wants you to live your life with that same creative power, bringing order to chaos. God's general will brings you to the place you're supposed to be. Yeah, it may look like a simple vessel, not flashy. Sure. But you'll need to battle an air of familiarity in it. Jesus wants you to be in the general will of God boat, because as you get in it and stay in it, you'll begin to find His specific will.

God's specific will is His next-level will. It doesn't come outside of knowing God's general will, but it comes and is heard within God's general will because it takes knowing God's general will to decipher His specific will. The disciples knew something about Jesus was special. They couldn't understand how He'd made all that food back there, and they didn't know why so many basketfuls were left over. The Bible says their hearts were hard. But special revelation—a special look into who Jesus was (and necessarily who they were in this whole story—men who would be called to Him, to take up His ministry)—came as they were obedient to His general will. Even Peter heard, "Come" from the boat.

Romans 12:2 says, "Do not conform to the pattern of this world" (as in, don't allow your will and future to be shaped by how the world defines success and direction), "but be transformed by the renewing of your mind" (NIV). Transformation of the mind happens by the Holy Spirit, through the Word of God, and within the context of relationships. It happens in the general will of God. The verse continues, "that you may prove what is that good and acceptable and perfect will of God" (NKJV).

We hear God's specific will as we have yielded to and been transformed by God's general will. But God's specific will appears a little more exciting than God's general will, and herein lies the dilemma. Sweet revelations about how amazing Jesus is and what

He can do (like watching His powerful word allow a friend to experience something impossible) seem way more fun than the day-to-day will of God. Especially to the outsider.

We all want to hear a prophetic word that tells us we're going to marry a dreamboat and who that person is (specific will). We'd prefer that over the long and agonizing process of becoming somebody worth marrying (general will) or being in the right place for all that to transpire.

The general will boat got all the disciples to the other side. It gets the job done. Even if you never have a prophetic word in your life, just do what you know the Bible tells you to do, work hard, develop your skills, and stay in community, and you'll absolutely be doing God's specific will without ever having necessarily "heard" it.

The general will of God is a hard place to be faithful and stay within because of how much faith it requires. People think walking on water requires a lot of faith, but Peter had *little* faith and was able to do it. The general will of God requires a lot of faith because of how often you must remind yourself it's what God wants. It becomes tedious and tiresome; we become ungrateful. Many—maybe most—Christians are in the boat, but they want to jump ship. For instance, they don't think their church is "speaking" to them anymore, so they wander away. God wants them to be planted so they can be fruitful (general will), but they have itching ears for something "special."

I have so much respect for people who don't abandon the boat and stay faithful to God's general will. Consider marriage. That's a general will boat all kinds of people jump out of, forgetting that

Jesus said, "What therefore God has joined together, let not man separate" (Mark 10:9). That's a *Get in the boat, stay in the boat* directive if I've ever heard one! But what if it gets stormy? *But it looks like the boat is going to capsize. I'm afraid! I'm angry! I'm discouraged! Where is Jesus?* He's coming. Stay in the boat. God told you to stay in the boat, so don't jump ship!

The dad who works at the factory, day in and day out, pouring out his life for his family, can be a hero of faith—if his work is simply surrendered in response to God. He's staying in the boat because God told him to through His general will. First Timothy 5:8 is brutal. It says, "If anyone does not provide for his relatives, and especially for members of his household, he has denied the faith and is worse than an unbeliever." That is a word from God for every provider. God has you in a boat that's keeping you faithful and self-sacrificing (hmm, that sounds like Jesus!), and you're crushing a faith life right now! You aren't living a small life; you're living a massive, obedient life of faith. You've heard God, and that's why you're in the boat.

In moments when we've forgotten why we're doing what we're doing in the first place, we need to come back to God's plain voice. *No, I'm here because I'm providing for my family. I prayed for this job and God came through. I used to be thankful for this opportunity to work, but I've become a little tired of it. Yet this job is a gift from God, and I'm called to it and graced for it. Until I hear otherwise, I'm going to keep doing what God has told me to do. God is good and faithful, and He leads and guides me. If He wanted me to have something else, I'd have it, because He's the*

Good Shepherd and I lack nothing that He wants me to have. I'm going to rehearse His good will in this place I'm in.

Isaiah 40:31 talks about how those who wait on the Lord shall renew their strength: "They will soar on wings like eagles; they will run and not grow weary, they will walk and not be faint" (NIV). The flashy parts of the verse are "wings like eagles" and "run and not grow weary," but the most day-to-day part is the "walk and not be faint." Most of life is walking, putting one foot in front of the other at an extremely slow pace. Most of life is monotonous, and yes, you can get tired and worn out from simply walking. Paul picks up on this theme when he writes to the Galatians. Galatians 6:9 reads, "Let us not grow weary of doing good." Getting tired of doing the right thing repeatedly is a real challenge. Never mind doing the bad things of life or the futile things of life and getting burned out on them. You can get tired of doing the right thing!

We must take up an attitude of faith when it comes to the good things that God has told us to do. We must treat these things as if they came from God's lips and not allow Scripture to become common. Conviction about God's general will is okay too! You can get stubborn about it! You can be, like, "This is *my* church, and I'm not going anywhere!"

What if we treated the boat that God has called us to like we treat our favorite football team? Think "Bills Mafia"—the die-hard fans of the Buffalo Bills, who not only have to live their lives in snowy Buffalo, New York, but also must cheer on a football club that hasn't loved them back in twenty-five years. But somehow, the Bills Mafia have become all the rage on Instagram lately. Their fans are certifiably *nuts*. They do crazy things to get themselves excited about the boat they're in. They jump off the backs of trucks onto food displays in the parking lot while they tailgate; they set themselves on fire and then jump off their trucks onto plastic tables. It's all part of whipping themselves into a believing *frenzy*. And we're talking about a small NFL franchise in a smaller, postindustrial town on the Canadian border.

What if we were like that as *Christians*? (Minus most of the jumping off stuff).

This is my *marriage, and I love my wife, and God gave her to me when I was a single loser without any prospects, and I'm called to* this *boat, and no matter what happens, I'm not jumping ship because* this is my boat! God told me to be in this boat ten years ago, and so I'm staying!

Or, *This is* my *job and God gave it to me when I prayed for a job, and I'm coming early and leaving late and loving every minute of it because God gave it to me, and until He says otherwise, I'm going to dominate it!*

What are some things you believe are your boat? What are some things you believe are God's general will for you? Write them down. Write down everything you believe God ordained. Think of His answers to prayer. What are they? Have you forgotten they are God's voice into your life—His shaping and leading and guiding? Are you treating them like that in your thoughts and feelings? Or have you forgotten that God brought you into these circumstances? Are you just looking for a way out because you feel tired and you're at the point where you could manipulate just about anything to seem like God's voice saying, *Go*?

Allow God's voice to come and confirm His leading, His guiding, and His hand on your life. Take some time to take stock of what He has already said and done. Write down all the ways He has spoken and confirmed His general will about the place you're in right now. What is the wisdom in staying where you are right now? Is God confirming things through the growth you've been experiencing? Or maybe it's time to go! Maybe God is saying, *Mission accomplished! You've stayed in the boat through the thick and thin, and now I'm telling you to take a little water walk with Me until we find another boat.* The water walk always leads back to a boat. God calls us to a people, a place, a purpose, and a provision. He doesn't call us to live flaky lives without planting or direction. He calls us to wisdom-filled lives of faith, where we're following His general will.

If God said it, you can do it!

 Remember: Faith is about hearing God both as part of a community and as an individual. And our wise response makes the difference between a life changed and disappointment. Be diligent in pursuing God's general will for your life.

CHAPTER TEN

The Myth of the Boring God

How to Get Ready for What You're Never Going to Be Ready For

When Jesus heard this, he was amazed and said to those following him, "Truly I tell you, I have not found anyone in Israel with such great faith."

—Matthew 8:10, NIV

Some years ago, I was hobbling around New York City like Crutchy from *Newsies*. I had a bad knee. Every time I took a step, I felt a sharp pain—like a fiery knife—shooting through my right leg. This went on for two years.

Aside from going to the doctor (I'm a man, and as such, we go to the doctor only when we're knockin' on heaven's door) I tried *everything*—right down to different shoes and insoles. I mean, I was twenty-nine. What healthy man wears insoles at *twenty-nine*? At one point, I found myself on that frustrating shoe insert machine at the store, trying desperately to figure out exactly which type to buy. I remember looking longingly at a pair of "grandma shoes"—Velcro closures and all. *Five-inch padded soles.* I drooled. *Grandma's walking on sunshine . . .*

Eventually, I called my dad.

"My knee is messed up," I said. "I need help."

"Go to the chiropractor."

"The chiropractor?"

"Yes."

"No."

"Yes."

"*No.* I am *not* going to that witch doctor, Dad." I huffed. "It's a soft science."

"Shut up, Nathan. He's awesome."

"He's a *garlic hanger.* I don't need voodoo! I need to have the thing lopped off by a pirate surgeon." Finally, I was ready to be more serious. "I'm in a lot of pain."

"Son," Dad said, "go to the chiropractor."

So I did. As I was sitting in his office, I told him about my knee, feeling like a total idiot. He touched it and stretched it. After about a minute he looked me in the eye and said, "Mr. Finochio, it seems like you have a tight IT band."

"Information technology band?"

"*Iliotibial band.* I want you to do a set of stretches every day. Two weeks, and you should be fine."

I limped out. *Stretches? Who does stretches? Stretches are for cheerleaders, not for manly men like me who have real problems in real life.* I knew I was wasting my time. But I went home and did my stretches, day after day. After a week, the pain was gone. That was five years ago. To this day, if I keep doing my stretches, no knee pain. When I stop, it comes back.

I had been so desperate that I was willing to see past my strange prejudices against chiropractors. Now I do everything he says, and I limp a lot less.

Hard to Hear

Sometimes God's breakthrough ideas come from people or places you don't want to have the answer for your question. Why? Well, *because God's not boring.* We often box Him in, telling ourselves we know all the ways He can and can't speak, work, or shape us. At that point we're setting ourselves up for a rough awakening. He loves to break our paradigms.

We all have prejudices. I find it difficult to listen to some people. Something about them just rubs me wrong. Sometimes it's petty, like their style of delivery. Sometimes I've heard them say something illogical or that I don't agree with, and then I shut down to anything else they have to say because I let the past color the present. Maybe it's their hair. Maybe it's their politics. Who knows? Who cares? It's a type of dismissal that journeys well beyond wise discernment and becomes personal prejudice.

But if I'm honest with myself, I realize that the only one who loses out in that scenario is *me.* Let's all be honest. If God wanted to use only perfect people, He wouldn't be able to use anyone— including you and me. But I persist in attempting to create this perfect scenario in which I'll hear God without being challenged or having my paradigms and assumptions stretched by less-than-perfect people.

He rarely lets that happen. *Because He is not boring.*

When I hear someone cherry-pick Bible verses out of context to make a point, I get angry: *How dare you come up in here and start acting the fool? That's not what that scripture is about— Paul is certainly not saying what you're trying to make him say. Where did you get this sermon—the toilet store? Where did you go to Bible college? Oh wait, you didn't. Let's see what's happening online, because I have twenty more minutes to endure this homiletical tragedy . . .*

I drop out and shut down. But you know what? No matter how bad it is, *I'm* the one who loses. How? Because God might have something to say to me, even if the source is less than perfect and my proud ears are plugged.

What a terrible attitude. And when I begin to think about all the reasons someone else shouldn't listen to *me*, well, let's just say it's *humbling*.

I wonder how many times I've missed something that could've been rocket fuel for transformation because I was too proud to listen to what wasn't coming from the place I wanted it to come from and the way I wanted it to come. No one is perfect. While we need standards for integrity and excellence for all of us, God used a donkey to speak to Balaam. He doesn't have the same standards we do—maybe because He sees every part of our hearts.

Do you really think all the God-words and good advice you need are going to come softly, kindly, graciously, and when you're "in a good place" to hear them? No, they're not! Look, when you're hungry, you'll eat. I don't want to get to a place where I'm not hungry when I go before God. I want to be so aware of my spiritual condition that I'm willing to listen to whoever is in front of me and "chew on the meat and spit out the bones." I will hear God better if I do, discerning through His Spirit what is real, what is fake, and what's in between.

Even having the perfect formula for God to speak into and through the good structures we've created a rhythm of life around can sometimes become sacred cows. We can have great theology and solid relationships and daily devotions and prophetic words and frequent getaways and retreats, and even *then* God will decide to speak in an unusual way just to mess with our paradigm and keep us on our toes.

Sometimes we get too comfortable in our rhythms. Spiritual pride can begin to set in because we think we have the corner on correct spirituality. We become very disciplined, and so we think God owes us. Or maybe we have attitudes toward others who haven't developed the disciplines of reading the Bible and prayer. We start to think we've got a direct line to heaven because we're so pious and obedient and self-sacrificing. Self-righteousness is a creepy thing that tends to grow on disciplines like ivy grows on sturdy old brick homes.

And yet the Bible is full of people who had to hear God through humbling, upside-down experiences.

Maybe sometimes God wants to speak to us, but we keep demanding that He speak through the ways we've become proud of. It's as if we tend to put God into a corner. *Well, Lord, if You're going to reach me, I know it'll be on my retreat.* Or *at the altar of this conference.* Or *when I fast next week.* Once again, these things are all good, but God's not a lip-reader; He's a heart-reader. And once again, the Bible says He resists the proud but "gives grace to the humble" (James 4:6; 1 Peter 5:5).

If you have spiritual pride, God will start to resist you. But nothing attracts Him to someone like humility. Humility before God is the proper estimation of one's own person and circumstance, God's person and circumstance, and the chasm between. It's a revelation from heaven that doesn't come from flesh and blood but from the Father. Either people receive it and respond in faith or they reject it and live in disbelief.

But honestly, this is such a human problem—this expectation for how God will speak that gradually morphs into prejudice. I want someone to show me what it looks like. Maybe you feel that way too.

Let's turn to the Bible with this in mind. Let's look at a couple of examples of this principle that God is likely to speak in the way we least expect, through the person we least wish. Only two people in the New Testament, according to Jesus, had "great faith." Just *two*. Unexpectedly for the pious and uptight Jews around Him, these two people were Gentiles. But they had a revelation from the Father about who Jesus was. They somehow had heard God. And their unexpected faith can teach us a lot about how God wants to speak to us today.

The Centurion

You can't talk about hearing God—about the source of all biblical faith—without talking about the centurion, who Jesus Himself said had the most faith in all of Israel. *What?* Let's read the story:

> When Jesus had entered Capernaum, a centurion came to him, asking for help. "Lord," he said, "my servant lies at home paralyzed, suffering terribly."
>
> Jesus said to him, "Shall I come and heal him?"

The centurion replied, "Lord, I do not deserve to have you come under my roof. But just say the word, and my servant will be healed. For I myself am a man under authority, with soldiers under me. I tell this one, 'Go,' and he goes; and that one, 'Come,' and he comes. I say to my servant, 'Do this,' and he does it."

When Jesus heard this, he was amazed and said to those following him, "Truly I tell you, I have not found anyone in Israel with such great faith." (Matthew 8:5–10, NIV)

Let that sink in. The most faith attributed to a single biblical character in the New Testament comes from a guy who is a "highly influential" Roman soldier, the upper echelon of society. Not only did Jesus not typically gravitate to this type of person (and especially not to Romans), but the centurion would never be expected to go to an itinerant, homeless rabbi for help. Talk about a tough place to find truth!

This time was tensely political for Jesus and the Romans. The Jewish people resented the Romans, and for Jesus to be seen with them was risky. To the Jews, the Romans were the bad guys; as a general rule they were occupiers and violent, exploiting others. So it's important to keep in mind that this Roman centurion had heard something about Jesus not necessarily directed *to* him. What he heard was something *over*heard—not *to* him but certainly *for* him.

The Bible is exactly like this today. It wasn't written *to* us, but it was certainly written *for* us. We weren't with Jesus when He preached to the crowds or healed people, but the message He preached and the stories about what He did for people are certainly for us. God's Word is so powerful that it can ricochet off others and hit us square in the eyes. What can be spoken to others can be for us as well. The state of our hearts—a desperate humility to receive things from God that were first given to others—is clearly a factor here for the centurion.

After hearing about Jesus healing people, the centurion had a decision to make. For us to understand the complexity of his response, we need to understand the political situation in Israel at the time a bit more: The Roman soldiers resented and despised both the Jewish people and the land. They were constantly having to quell violent uprisings, and they resented how religiously zealous and sectarian the Jews were, which was all so complicated and alien to their mostly easygoing religions. They disliked the weather and culture as well. Much of the culture was tense, strict, and socially strange to them. The Jews equally resented and despised the Romans because they were occupiers of their beloved nation. And with the Romans came their evil, violent, "unclean," and corrupting foreign practices that swayed some of the Jewish people.

The centurion had to overcome his own sense of national pride and racial prejudice to reach out to this Jewish prophet. And even then would be uncertainty. What if Jesus hated the Romans? What if this Jesus of Nazareth mocked him in front of the crowds? Or what if the centurion's comrades in arms found out he was seeking help from a Jewish healer? The whole interaction would have been anxiety inducing because of the probability of a disastrous outcome.

We gather that the centurion really loves his servant because he's willing to overcome all his pride for even the chance of his restoration. So we see the centurion come to Jesus, calling Him "Lord" and appealing to Him in a way unbefitting a Roman officer. It's stunning.

The centurion's natural eyes told him that the authority structures of Rome—the prominence, elegance, Roman sophistication, and regal airs of power he was so accustomed to knowing and honoring and fighting for—were completely absent in the person of this Jesus. Nothing about Jesus was great or prestigious. The truth is that the greatest faith doesn't come without its tainted lens of human experience.

We so often think others are broken, and sometimes they are. But as the old saying goes, "Even a broken clock is right twice a day." And guess what. God uses broken clocks. A lot of them.

We never stop seeing in the natural. We have our prejudices and preferences about who will say what and do what. That's what's so difficult about a faith life! We must continue to go back to what we've heard and allow that to set our course, rather than reacting to what we see. Desperation of circumstance and heart helps us with that. Jesus said, "Blessed are those who hunger and thirst for righteousness, for they shall be filled" (Matthew 5:6, NKJV). People who are hungry and thirsty for God's voice hear God's voice. God responds to hunger, which means we must stay hungry.

In many ways we need to get past what we see, especially in others God is using to speak to us. We're all centurions who have a certain expectation of where and how material power structures will manifest themselves for us and break through on our behalf.

We will struggle in the dark to find the explosive Word of God for our lives—the living Word that brings world-shaking faith. The paradox of the clean God is that He heals in muddy waters so that all glory is brought to Him alone.

We consider people and circumstances in the flesh all the time, and we lose heaven because we want the victory to come from a place of human glory. Spiritual authority is absolutely a gateway from God that delivers His word consistently. But hard circumstances—like the boat in the storm where the disciples found themselves, like that soul-crushing job God has called us to be faithful in, or like that marriage that seems more like Space Mountain than the Little Mermaid attraction at Disney World— are the places where God is always glorified. Death should come from these places, and yet He brings life through them.

The centurion possessed a decided simplicity concerning the origin of Jesus's power. He understood chain of command, and that power has a beginning place and must necessarily come through channels for its distribution. He got the point and responded in true faith to what he heard.

The centurion saw past his prejudiced vision to a fountain of power flowing through this unlikely man, Jesus. We must learn to do the same. We must get back to centurion hearing—a kind of hearing that recognizes its prejudices to move *past* its prejudices; a hearing that's so motivated by love for others that it will humble itself to the point of a complete emptying of social positioning or economic ordering. You aren't just hearing God for you; you're hearing God for others! Faith breeds faith.

The Canaanite Woman

This story is wild. Let's read it.

> A Canaanite woman from that vicinity came to him,
> crying out, "Lord, Son of David, have mercy on me! My
> daughter is demon-possessed and suffering terribly."
>
> Jesus did not answer a word. So his disciples came to
> him and urged him, "Send her away, for she keeps crying
> out after us."
>
> He answered, "I was sent only to the lost sheep of
> Israel."
>
> The woman came and knelt before him. "Lord, help
> me!" she said.
>
> He replied, "It is not right to take the children's bread
> and toss it to the dogs."
>
> "Yes it is, Lord," she said. "Even the dogs eat the
> crumbs that fall from their master's table."
>
> Then Jesus said to her, "Woman, you have great faith!
> Your request is granted." And her daughter was healed at
> that moment. (Matthew 15:22–28, NIV)

I mean, Jesus is straight *savage* to this woman whose daughter
is demon possessed. Once again, we see someone seeking Jesus for
someone else. She'll do anything for her daughter. She's desperate
for her to be made well.

This woman wasn't Jewish, and she would've been so aware of

how little status and respect she had in this culture. Gentiles were disliked, but Gentile women were despised. For this woman to call after Jesus in public, she had to be next-level desperate. She was risking a lot. She was humble, and she was hungry for what only Jesus could bring: healing.

Because of that, because she wants to hear healing from God *so badly,* she's willing to go to the last place in the world she would expect to find mercy.

She calls out, "Lord, Son of David, have mercy on me!" Notice that she addresses Jesus by His *messianic* title, Son of David. This woman doesn't just know about what Jesus is doing; she knows who He is. She's not only appealing to His ability; she's appealing to His power, seen only through genuine faith. Matthew is making a point here to his Jewish readers: even Gentiles recognize who Jesus is, so how much more readily should Jews recognize His messianic identity and thus His ability to heal and restore and save?

His disciples are, like, "Jesus, send her away. She keeps shouting at us." This woman is putting it all on the line, totally humbling herself because she has no other options. She knows her only shot at her daughter's restoration is directly in front of her, telling her, "Sorry, this isn't for you." That's *faith*—her willingness to hear God speak despite so many reasons she should dismiss it. She isn't budging; she isn't getting quieter. She's annoying the daylights out of the disciples and probably Jesus. But remember, this persistence is how Jesus taught us to pray in that parable about the persistent widow in Luke 18:1–8. Maybe this woman was the inspiration for that one, telling us we should barrage God with our prayers.

What are you like when you've heard something from God, when you think the Holy Spirit has given you a word or a revelation about Jesus? Do you persist in prayer? Or are you a bit too casual? Do you give up, because deep down you believe this isn't for you?

Jesus says, "I was sent only to the lost sheep of Israel." The woman bows down before Him, and she says again, "Lord, help me!" Jesus says, "It is not right to take the children's bread and toss it to the dogs."

What . . .

What the . . .

Meek and Kind and Gentle Jesus said *that* to a desperate woman begging Him for a miracle? (What the actual what is going on?)

Talk about totally not "seeker sensitive." Jesus is giving this woman every reason to stop following Him, to be disheartened. But He's also teaching a case lesson to His Jewish onlookers. Jesus knew her faith was so great that absolutely nothing was going to turn her off, so He used it as a teachable moment. Once again, pay attention to what Jesus says here. He's not on mission to her; He's on mission to them. It's costing her way more to be up in this Jesus game, shouting down Him and His crew like a crazy lady, than it's costing the Israelites, who are casually taking it all in. She's not welcomed. She stays anyway. She persists.

Listen to how she responds to Jesus: "Yes it is, Lord. . . . Even the dogs eat the crumbs that fall from their master's table."

Wow. Heavy. And heartfelt. *Yes, I'm as good as a dog in this circumstance.* That's what she's saying. *I'm the dog in this metaphor, not even to be considered the child.* Now, that is the kind of humility that hears God and gets miracles. *But even the dogs get the crumbs from the floor.*

Then Jesus says, "Woman, you have great faith! Your request is granted." And at once her daughter is healed.

Humble and Hungry

A Roman soldier who had to overcome his own prejudice and a Canaanite woman who had to overcome prejudice against her are two people who love so deeply that they'll do anything for someone else. They're two people whose faith led them to hear God where they likely least expected it—from the carpenter from Nazareth.

The faith Jesus admires isn't dismissive of where God's voice is coming from; it doesn't write off people or situations. This is why faith is so tied with spiritual maturity, and to the whole idea that Jesus gives more to the person who already has something (Matthew 25). Why? Because humility breeds maturity breeds humility. It's the best of cycles. God speaks. *If* we listen, we grow. If we grow, we hear Him better next time. But hope is found in the truth that it's never too late to start listening for Him where we least expect to hear anything.

God has much to say to us, but hearing His voice may come from places we just never dreamed. And there's the crazy thing—

we will never be ready for where it's coming from next. It will be consistent with His character, and it will be consistent with the revelation He's already given us, but at its core it will likely carry the element of surprise and demand that we humble ourselves to receive it.

God likes to see what's under the hood, so to speak. He gets to the inner motivations and attitudes that drive us. He's a heart-reader. He's looking to see if there's some hunger and thirst. And He will absolutely speak in ways that will require our humility to hear.

Humility brings healing. It's what Jesus responds to. Great faith is an act of humility every time because it puts no confidence in the flesh but rather in the speaking God who can perform His word no matter the situation.

God might use a humbling experience to speak to you. He might use your brother who annoys you or your sister who always talks down to you. Tough rocks. If God uses you and you're imperfect, He'll use someone else who's imperfect.

To speak to you, God might use a friend who's always up in your business and calling you on stuff. That friend might come off a little this or that, but God might have something to say through that friend. Look past the flesh. Are you hungry? Are you open to receive?

Ask the Holy Spirit to make you hungry for truth—no matter where it comes from—and to speak to you. Our prayer should become, *God, make me hungry and humble.* If we're hungry and humble, God will show up. I want to be so hungry for God's words that I don't care who cooked it or what plate it's coming on!

Lord, make me hungry. Make me humble.
Help me be ready for what I'm never going to be ready for.
Hearing You.

Remember: God speaks to us in ways
we would never expect. Only humility
lets us hear Him when He does.

Conclusion

Like so many paradoxes of faith, listening for God's voice is the kind of thing you can't force. You can't manufacture it. All you can do is learn to lean in, work to wait, be hungry for humility, and respond to what you have.

The truth is that we're listening all the time. We're guided all the time. We're receiving all the time. Just as it's almost impossible to watch grass grow with your naked eye, yet a time-lapse video reveals all *sorts* of growth, our perception of our progress in listening can be discouraging. Sure, some people seem like bamboo— springing up feet per day. But you know what? You're responsible for how you hear God in your unique circumstances. And that is a gift.

Here's the practical truth: if we know the Scriptures, have the right people around us, and cooperate with what the Bible and our godly friends tend to say, it's going to be tough *not* to hear God. Together, the Bible and godly relationships will act like a mirror so we'll know exactly what reality is. Without the Bible and godly relationships, we have no concept of what's truly real. Reality is what corresponds with the truth.

As Christians, we're called to treasure God's Word and God's people. As we continue to be faithful with what we're given (whether that's a ton or tiny bit), we can be confident that the Spirit of God will be faithful to lead and guide our lives, until Jesus returns.

In the end, we can be confident that we have heard God. That we *are* hearing Him. And that we *will* hear Him. His promises are sure. His Spirit is faithful. His people are here and present. His Word is available.

In responding, we will grow, inch by inch, more into the image of Jesus.

And if that isn't the point of this whole life, what is?

Because as we change how we listen, we are changed more into His likeness.

Praise God!

Response Ideas

If you want to take next steps in hearing God for yourself, consider these practical ideas to get your listening started.

Chapter One—The Myth of Easy Conversation

When's the last time you asked the Holy Spirit to fill you? Plan to cultivate a Holy Spirit atmosphere in your life this week. Maybe that means going for a walk and listening to some worship music, and rather than passively listening to the music, asking the Holy Spirit to meet you and fill you in that time. Commit to ten solid minutes of prayer and worship, thanking the Holy Spirit for His fresh work in your life today.

Chapter Two—The Myth of Technicolor Holy Spirit Wonkaland

Who does God want you to be? I'm not talking about what God wants you to do; I'm talking about what He wants you to be. Have you ever felt as though God has spoken to your heart about how He wants you to be, and who that type of person (Jesus, ahem) would look like? Make a list of things you believe God has been "highlighting" in your life—places of character you think His voice is speaking to. When you're done, thank God for His powerful Holy Spirit, who is giving you the grace to be who you are called to be so you can do what you're called to do.

Chapter Three—The Myth of Hunky-Dory La-La Land

Have you been carrying any assumptions about the devil, his demons, and their power over your life? Ask God to let the truth about His power set you free from needless and unfounded fear and superstition so you can walk in full assurance and confidence that He—and nobody else!—is in charge of your life.

Chapter Four—The Myth of the Easy Book

Do you believe the Bible is God's Word? If so, are you giving yourself to becoming a better listener to His Word? Plan to learn more about the Bible, especially how to study it, maybe with an online class or in a study group at your local church. Either way, plan today to grow in your ability to handle God's Word.

Chapter Five—The Myth of the Lone Ranger Christian

Who are some people in your life you consider to have godly wisdom? When's the last time you asked them for wisdom? Are you doing your part in knocking on heaven's door for wisdom? Plan to reach out to a potential mentor this week, or to rekindle a mentoring relationship that may have grown cold.

Chapter Six—The Myth of "Don't Worry! Nothing Weird Will Happen!"

When's the last time you encouraged someone? When's the last time someone encouraged you? Become a prophetic person and you'll attract prophetic people. Plan this week to get around someone with a prophetic gift and put a demand on the gift of God inside you. Also, encourage *them*!

Chapter Seven—The Myth of Disposable Nature

Are you neglecting areas of rest in your life? What are they? Make a list of what gives your soul rest. Now make a plan to begin restoring balance. Ask the Holy Spirit to help you. He wants your soul to be restored so He can get your attention. He can't speak much to you if you're always just barely surviving on life support.

Chapter Eight—The Myth of Greener Grasses

Do you feel called where you are? Do you remember if the Holy Spirit confirmed that you were supposed to be where you are? List some of His leading and confirmations this week. Refresh yourself in His faithfulness. Do you feel stirred to go somewhere else? Make a list of these stirrings. Submit them to a close friend or mentor who is full of the Holy Spirit and has godly wisdom.

Chapter Nine—The Myth of Solid Water

Do you have a profound sense of calling to a relationship or to your church or to what you're pursuing in work or vocation? Do you even view it as a calling? Or do you see it as more happenstance? Can you point back to moments and words where the Holy Spirit confirmed some vital areas of your life? You can have faith for those things! You can pray into these areas passionately, knowing that God is the one calling you. Pray, believing that the best is yet to come. Faith is not blind optimism; it's a response to God's promise-keeping words!

Chapter Ten—The Myth of the Boring God

What are "stretches" in your life you know God speaks and works through? Maybe it's daily devotions, or maybe it's discipline in an area you tend to let go to the wayside. Maybe you've been trying to do things on your own, and God is desiring to "draw near" to you in a fresh way, and a little bit of humility would attract His voice. God resists the proud. Make a list of some possible places where you may have been resisting the grace of God because you can't stand the form of grace. Maybe it's something as practical as the gym, and God wants to speak to you in a profound way about the mechanics of perseverance through a trainer! Maybe it's through a book you can't stand because the author annoys you. We can rest in a powerful confidence anytime we humble ourselves because humility is the soil for spiritual growth.

Acknowledgments

My thanks go to the following:

My wife, Jasmine, who has been the most supportive voice around this project.

Joel Houston, who continually fans the flames in his friends. So much of this book was bounced off Joel when I would rudely interrupt his lyric-writing sessions on the back porch of the studio for some feedback.

Frank Damazio, who told me I would write.

My brother, Gabriel, my harshest critic and most loyal ally.

My parents, who are prouder than punch.

Steve and Fiona Edwards, for their encouragement and support.

Andrew Stoddard, for believing in me and being so genuine.

Whitney Gossett, who is more available to me and positive than any human being. How do you do it?

Paul Pastor, a true genius, for working tirelessly and guiding my crazy into clarity.

Bryan and Tiffany, for making Frankie. I love you both.

Amy and Samuel, for being my favorites.

David and Alana Kuwabara, who prophesied this book over me and have been my best friends over the longest haul.

And to Natalie, Austin, Jeremy, Lois, Renae, Nate, Kayla, Dylan, Lindsay, Lozzie (Caviar), Andrew, Janice, Crocker,

Brea, Esther, Izzy, Davs, Kimes, Kane, John, Joe, Kelia, Justin, Hailey, Beidels, Double D, Dennis Lacheney, Andrew, Julia, Skinny Dennis, Casa Migos, Humphrey Bogart, George Harrison, Stevie Wonder, Australia, dollar-slice pizza—thank you!

Notes

1. Jordan B. Peterson, *Maps of Meaning: The Architecture of Belief* (Abington, UK: Routledge, 1999), 81.
2. G. K. Chesterton, "The Ethics of Elfland," in *The Collected Works of G. K. Chesterton,* vol. 1, *Orthodoxy* (San Francisco: Ignatius, 1986), 264.
3. William Shakespeare, *Macbeth* (New York: Living Shakespeare Inc., 1962), 5.
4. John Foxe, *Fox's Book of Martyrs: A History of the Lives, Sufferings, and Triumphant Deaths of the Early Christian and Protestant Martyrs,* ed. William Byron Forbrush (Philadelphia: John C. Winston, 1926).
5. David Hume, *A Treatise of Human Nature* (Oxford: Clarendon Press, 1888).
6. G. K. Chesterton, *The Collected Works of G. K. Chesterton,* vol. 3, *The Thing: Why I Am a Catholic* (San Francisco: Ignatius, 1986), 131.
7. Bruce Waltke, *An Old Testament Theology: An Exegetical, Canonical, and Thematic Approach* (Grand Rapids, MI: Zondervan, 2007), 58.
8. A. W. Tozer, *Man: The Dwelling Place of God; What It Means to Have Christ Living in You* (Camp Hill, PA: WingSpread, 1997), 66.
9. G. K. Chesterton, *The Collected Works of G. K. Chesterton,* vol. 21, *The Resurrection of Rome* (San Francisco: Ignatius, 1986).

10. C. S. Lewis, *Surprised by Joy: The Shape of My Early Life* (Orlando, FL: Harcourt, 1966), 207–8.

11. R. D. Shaw, "The First Epistle to the Corinthians," in *The International Standard Bible Encyclopedia,* ed. James Orr (Chicago: Howard-Severance, 1915), 713.

12. Saint Thomas Aquinas, *The Aquinas Catechism: A Simplified Explanation of the Catholic Faith by the Church's Greatest Theologian* (Manchester, NH: Sophia Institute, 2000), 71.

13. G. K. Chesterton, *The Collected Works of G. K. Chesterton,* vol. 1, *Heretics* (San Francisco: Ignatius, 1986), 72.

14. Edward Hickman, ed., *The Works of Jonathan Edwards,* vol. 1 (Edinburgh: Banner of Truth Trust, 1974), 47.

15. C. S. Lewis, *Mere Christianity* (San Francisco: HarperOne, 2015), 28–29.

16. Scott Olster, "Bill Gates' Very Full Life After Microsoft," June 21, 2010, *Fortune,* http://fortune.com/2010/06/21/bill-gates-very-full-life-after-microsoft.

17. G. K. Chesterton, "On Mr. Rudyard Kipling and Making the World Small," *The Collected Works of G. K. Chesterton,* vol. 1, *Heretics* (San Francisco: Ignatius, 1986), 60.

18. Chesterton, *Heretics,* 60.

19. *Lexham Analytical Lexicon to the Greek New Testament,* s.v. "anankazo."

20. Philip H. Towner, "Will of God," in *Baker's Evangelical Dictionary of Biblical Theology,* ed. Walter A. Elwell (Grand Rapids, MI: Baker, 1997).